Feet Upon The Earth
The Ordinary Person's Guide to Seeking an Extraordinary Life

based on
My Healing Journey with Spirit Guides and Past Lives

By
Louise M. Mitchell

AuthorHouse™
1663 Liberty Drive
Bloomington, IN 47403
www.authorhouse.com
Phone: 1-800-839-8640

First published by AuthorHouse 09/12/2011

ISBN: 978-1-4634-2879-2 (sc)
ISBN: 978-1-4634-2880-8 (ebk)
ISBN: 978-1-4634-2881-5 (hc)

Library of Congress Control Number: 2011911669

Printed in the United States of America

This book is printed on acid-free paper.

Cover art:
Surrealism (Image ID #3695476) © Yuran / Crestock
Broken Heart (Image ID #2956382) © olalundqvist / Crestock
Drops on the web (Image ID #3271019) © vblinov / Crestock
Mountain lion (Image ID #3513789) © visceralimage / Crestock
Interior art:
Morning dew on spider web (Image ID #1095391) © Laures / Crestock
Rock path through the forest (Image ID #158) © salanskt / Crestock

For Jim and Matt,
It *is* a great forever.

Acknowledgements,

Sara

Sandra T. Ridgely, Editor

Critique Group and Members of
Mountain Writers

"Behind the face you often show the world,
Is a happier face."

Contents

Preface

Meditation, Spirit Guides, and Past Lives

Meditation has been my pathway in seeking answers to the question "Is there more to life than the visible, tangible world around me? Is there more that is invisible?" Most people today are familiar with some form of meditation—be it sitting, lying down, walking, indoors, outdoors, casual, formal, ceremonial, guided, in groups, or solitary. My meditations are visionary and the guided substance of my journey. In this book, you will find that meditations reveal captivating stories that bring awareness, growth, wisdom, and healing, as well as answers to the question of *more*.

Spirit Guides, or Guides, may be less known to you. Throughout life, Spirit Guides wait to assist us in seeking answers to the big questions, to uncovering our identity, and to moving us through lessons of the soul toward wholeness, Oneness, and spiritual enlightenment. Guides are our protectors and nurturers. They poke us to notice something important, wink at us like flashing lights to get our attention, and whisper to us in dreams and meditations.

Guides represent different aspects of our true identity, our personal power, and our path in life. They provide support, opportunity, and energy to help us find our power, become comfortable with our power, and use our power for our own highest good.

They know us better than we know ourselves. They know what our purposes are, why we do the things we do, and why we do not do the things we could do. They know our fears and self-doubts, our feelings of powerlessness and confusion, anger and disappointment.

Living on the other side of a veil of consciousness, Guides know our relationship with suffering. They know the scars and wounds we carry. Most importantly, they say, we carry these scars, not for the purpose of continued suffering, but for the purpose of healing.

Reincarnation. A question I commonly receive is, "Do you believe in reincarnation?" This is a defining question that usually comes from people for whom that door has not yet swung open. My answer is, *yes, I believe in reincarnation,* and the more complete answer is, *I do not simply believe in it, I know I have lived many lives on Earth.* I took the challenge of looking within myself, delving deep into the inner corners of my being—like a dolphin swimming the oceans—and discovered who I am and who I have been. Some of these stories lay just beneath the surface.

My Guides have known me for many lifetimes. They have existed over the ages with me and awaited my invitation to be in relationship.

The consciousness on the planet is rising. Other people, too, are awakening and discovering the support and assistance offered by the Guides. If Earth is a schoolroom for the human race, we must master the lessons with which our Spirit Guides are here to assist.

It is said that when we know and resolve the roles we have played in the past—as men, women, and children of various races on different continents in different centuries—we may indeed be ready for enlightenment.

A Teacher's Guidance

On this journey, I made new friends, laughed, and played along the way, and studied and worked with healers and teachers. One wise person that crossed paths with me was a South American rainforest specialist and shaman who I will refer to as Condor. I call him wise, because he helped me to strengthen the spiritual connection I already had and to stay true to myself.

Condor is a dreamer and storyteller—humorous and dramatic, insightful and honest. During my studies with him in 1999, he greeted me at the door one day with his usual slow shuffle that said,

"I'm-from-the-hot-rainforest-where-no-one-rushes-like-you-busy-North Americans," but I sensed he urgently wanted to talk with me. We sat together—shaman teacher and student—and his story unfolded.

He said he had dreamed me. In the dream, I called to him, "Condor, Condor, come look." I had something to show him. So, he followed me up a mountain to a rock where I sat down. Near me he saw a Native American female elder. Addressing me by my Native American name, he asked, "Ah, who is she, Laughing Waters?" I would not tell him, so he went over to her and asked her name. She would not tell him. He did not understand. He said I looked at him smugly, as if I were sharing a secret with him. He was intrigued and continued to look at what was before him in this dream.

"You would not tell me her name," Condor recounted, "so I studied what I saw to try to understand. Between the two of you, I saw a single thread, like a spider's strand, connecting from the elder to the little finger of your left hand. What is this connection, I wondered? So, I went over and touched it. It was resilient and strong. I tried to break it. With all my strength, I could not break it. I tried repeatedly. Therefore, I realized you are connected to this Spirit woman. The connection is so fine, so delicate, my Laughing Waters, yet it is also strong, strong as steel. This connection with Spirit cannot be broken."

Condor concluded, "You do not need to study with me to learn to be a shaman like those in the South American rainforest. You already are connected to Spirit. In your meditations, climb the thread that connects you to the Source. Retrieve the energy and messages. Climb back down your thread into your body to Earthly life and share what you have learned. You are a Spider Woman, a writer who travels the web of life. Explore and find the message. Tell your story. This is the dream that lives in you. You can manifest your dream. Look within and there it will be."

This Book is Born

Look within and there it will be. So, I, a Spider Woman, explored and explored, and the truth is, there is a lot to learn—there *is* more to life than meets the eye. This journey has taken me across the web of life, woven of silver cord between Earth and Sun, spanning all time and all places, glistening and trembling where I have lived.

My Guides urged me to write about this journey for you. Condor dreamed it, too. It is not always easy to learn new things, grow and adapt, revise and rebuild our lives, but the idea of embarking on an expansive spiritual journey to create the most value and joy possible in life is irresistible. What a thrill it has been!

In this book in three parts, I introduce you to the leading cast of characters—my three Spirit Guides and myself. Then we visit past lives and learn the lesson, wisdom, or healing needed from each of those memories. The journey climaxes with arriving Home! Throughout the book, my Spirit Guide George contributes discourse that appears in indented paragraphs and narrations in Interludes between chapters.

My wish is that the story of the transformation of Laughing Waters leads you to find learning and peace beyond anything you have imagined, and that your heart soars freely.

When you have read this book, you will know that it is for you that I lived and learned.

Thank you.

PART I
STEPPING ONTO THE SACRED PATH

1

Ice Breaker
Spirit Guide George

There is a pathway to the Light. The doorway is inside you.
Find the key and the journey begins.

THERE HAS GOT TO BE more to life than this. What am I looking for?
Not food, shelter, or clothing, nor partner or friends. It is something
else that eludes me. If I tried to describe the feeling I have, it would
be inner confusion seeking understanding.

My life seems transient. Friends come and go. Neighbors move
away. Children graduate and move on. Projects start and end. There
is always flux and change, yet something in my life remains. How
do I define myself? The constant part of me must be *what*? If I am
not the sum total of my experiences, then what am I? And what am
I doing?

The joy of communing with nature is an inner hunger so strong
that I cannot continue to ignore it. The serenity of a walk in the
woods, the crashing excitement of a gushing waterfall, the natural
opening to full blossom of a brightly colored flower, the urge to walk
on boulders *in* the creek, the pure essence of a snowfall—all call
to me.

These were my thoughts and experiences that led me to meditation
where the answers to my questions revealed themselves. I had visions

and insights and met my Spirit Guides who led me through the challenges and rewards of my spiritual path.

My first challenge came in a meditation where I met my Spirit Guide George and observed my own struggle with defensiveness and an inner desire for peace. I recall the meditation, as if it were this morning:

She stood next to the partially frozen creek deciphering the images on the other side—a figure and an animal in the light and warmth of a crackling campfire. The creek water, frozen at the surface where it touched the cold air, gurgled slowly underneath. *Who was this curious man and donkey?* She was compelled, drawn to them. He was bearded and rough, both his skin and the fabrics of his worn clothing.

While intrigued and in need of refuge, she turned away to walk on. He had not indicated his awareness of her until she turned to go, when he moved to face her and beckon her across the waters to sit by his fire.

She complied and as she sat by the fire, the warm aura that she stepped into was refuge from the cold and seeped deep inside her. The warmth of the fire and the generous man who shared it filled the empty places and soothed over the troubled places in her. The joy of Oneness for which she had ached overtook her.

These feelings confused her. He sensed her discomfort and knew he must speak to keep her there. Eyeing her slyly, he said, "I knew you'd find me." Snapped from her reverie, she jumped to flee from these words and him. He added, "I've waited for you to seek me out your whole life."

"I'm not seeking you," she spat defensively. "I stumbled across you. You're a surprise to me. I do not know you. How could you know me?"

She left the aura of the campfire and walked across the snow in a bit of a huff. *This was predictable*, he chuckled knowingly to himself. *Yes, this was her personality!*

He moved quickly too, so when she was safely on the other side of the creek and turned to glance back at this strange aberration, he stood by the creek with his hands cupped together out in front of him.

She was angry over the closeness and familiarity of this stranger. He knew how she felt, and said "I have a gift for you."

"What is it?" she replied sarcastically. "Some rock from this river? I don't need another rock."

He tolerated her impolite response because he knew her—better than she knew herself. He did not relent with his offer of the gift. Not swayed by her demeanor, he stood strong against her onslaught like one of the deeply-rooted trees in the surrounding forest.

In her anger and confusion, she paced around the uneven, rocky river's edge in her own snit. She became aware of feeling fire in her as if flames of anger were consuming her. He waited out her reaction. She climbed some large boulders to the top of the ice-clad waterfall. Exhausted from her effort and rage, she stood looking out over the waterfall, the forest, the rocks, and the little vagabond man relentlessly holding his hands in offering to her. Her chest heaved from exertion and she breathed deeply to catch her breath.

When her breathing calmed, she relaxed and surveyed the scene with a quieter mind. In her head she heard the words, "He has a gift for you." *Yes*, she thought, *I already know this.* "The gift is for you," the voice encouraged. She followed this inner voice and slipped down to the riverbed's edge and stood across from the woodland intruder. She was guarded and not willing to be impressed by this poor man's gift.

Nonetheless, she stood attentively. He slowly opened the hiding place and from his hands flew a bird. While the bird flapped and flew and picked a safe distant spot to alight where it would not be held captive again, she thought, *well, at least it is not a rock. It is a bird*, she reflected. *What kind of bird?* As it landed, she spied a sparrow—an ordinary brown molten sparrow. Not a hawk or eagle, but an infuriatingly ordinary sparrow!

She was not grateful for this lowly gift and stormed back to her higher perch by the waterfall. The inner voice informed her, "It is the gift of freedom."

Huh? That got her attention. She stared over at the little ordinary bird perched on a soft limb of the highest hemlock. *Ordinary bird, extraordinary gift?* She sat and allowed her mind to flow with the experience.

As night fell, she moved to the warmth of the fire. The vagabond welcomed her. His wait for her was over. He nourished her Spirit and nurtured her healing with the warmth of the fire, his food, and his good company. "I will tell you a story," he said.

As someone who lives in the forest and wanders with all his possessions on the back of a mule, you think you know something that I need to know? More sarcasm. However, the warmth of love emanating from him and his fire was filling every cell of her being and flowing out from her empty spaces. She was in ecstasy. She and her sarcastic, know-it-all attitude stayed for George's story. Her hunger for answers led her to this place of surrender where the ice melts.

In the cold winter forest, snow and ice pellets fell intermittently as the wind blew. She remained warm outside and in, through and through, sustained by his energy and seemingly lost in time. She had ached for the experience of true fulfillment, and with the hermit who had a mule and a bird in his hands, she felt it. In his company, she did not need extra layers of protection from harsh elements.

He taught her, "Do not hold on to all of life's experiences. Learn from them and hold onto the wisdom and joy you gain. Let the experiences go. Feed your highest potential and push yourself up through the muck to the highest essence you can reach. See through the outer façade to the true value of your incarnation and make your life a joy of accomplishments that sets you free."

This introduction to my Spirit Guide George gave me an experience of witnessing the attitude with which I meet new experiences in life. His roughness was a reflection of my roughness, his lonely existence was the broken isolation of my existence, frozen waters were the unsure feelings and reluctance of my heart, and the sharp words, my fear. He is quite a storyteller, engaging and wise. George lives the life of a hermit, similar to the life of many writers—surrounded by solitude and self-reflective. In this way, we are similar.

GEORGE: Let me introduce myself. I am George. I live as a hermit in the wilderness, deep in the woods. I'm bearded and ragged in rawhide clothing. My pack mule is my only companion. I am short and stocky. My existence is perfect. I am a Spirit Guide for the woman, Louise. My love for her is total.

I roam the wild places, gathering the energy of the Earth for her. Many aspects of modern living deplete her, because they lack the charge of Earth energy. The natural Earth energies that I drape around her shoulders bring her home to the Earth. When she sees a bird take flight now, even a sparrow, she is reminded of her own personal freedom. I help her schedule time for walking, hiking, camping, and other solitary activities in the outdoors.

When she is close to the forest, she is close to me and the wonderful Earth energy. The campfires I build each night stoke the warmth of love, so she can learn to feel love and fill up on it to share with her family, friends, and all she touches. The power her soul carries is so strong that she must heal and carry an open, loving heart before she can use her power. An open heart flows with compassion for everyone, and receives the flow of love from others. Her heart began to open when we first met in this meditation.

George's Teaching: The Tao of Porcupine

On my first visit through Rocky Mountain National Park in Colorado, I made the entire drive without seeing any of the major-sized wildlife. Only pikas and marmots populated the scenic vista areas. I was interpreting this as an empty experience, when, suddenly, I had to brake for a slow porcupine waddling across the road. Another little mammal! He had made it past the centerline and was crossing my lane to reach the other side of the road. Interesting, because we were surrounded by miles and miles and miles of habitat, and he chose the highway. I did appreciate these little guys, but I was searching for something ... else.

Subsequently, the grander, more spectacular wildlife appeared out of the forests and in the meadows near rivers, but that porcupine remained a firm image in my mind.

Now, I get it! The porcupine was one of my beginning spiritual lessons. It has taken time, but George is teaching me to be more like porcupine: to develop and rely on trust and faith as my protection, to know my body is protected, and to open to others through playfulness and innocence. Transform my sharpness—of wit and words—and harm no one, unless truly threatened. When I sense the possibility of impending danger, I can picture porcupine waddling across the road and remind myself to approach the situation with a more playful attitude.

Spirit Guide George
Shield

2

See Your Reflection
Spirit Guide Still Waters

Retreat within to find the pictures of your Spirit.

MY GUIDE STILL WATERS IS not as talkative as George is, as you will see, and when she does speak, I drink up every word. Her messages are like cool drinks of water on a hot, parched day. She quenches thirst and is the ladle that pours water on the inner fire that burns too hot.

Still Waters helps me with female things and with my heart, home, and garden—she mothers me and works on opening my heart, so it is a clear, safe place from which to *feel*. She teaches me about the use of herbs for healing and the value of a calm, flowing, loving heart.

My first identifiable contact with Still Waters occurred following my fireside meditation with George. I drove my car on a road that went downhill and uphill. My mind was absorbed in nothing in particular. A female voice whispered over my left shoulder directly into my ear, "Louise is Laughing Waters." In the magic of Still Waters' lyrical voice, I could hear water gurgling and lapping across river stones in the sound of my name. I was tickled down to my toes! I was bestowed my Native American name! I was still grinning from ear to ear when, in a serendipitous coincidence, the two-lane,

9

meandering road went through a wooded park and crossed a dam with a still, deep reservoir to the left and a running creek to the right. The moment is clear in my memory and a highlight of my spiritual journey. I earned my Indian name that connects me to the Earth and I *loved* it! It is me.

I have heard Still Waters at other times, too. I was procrastinating about vacuuming the house one day and Still Waters whispered, "Sweep the hogan." The voice and message were like electric shock. *I wouldn't mind sweeping the hogan*, I thought. Great motivational trick, Still Waters! Oh, the nostalgia of stepping in leather moccasins on the dirt of the earth and living simply again!

On another occasion, I asked no one in particular, "Just how old am I?" The answer came from Still Waters, "Old as dirt!" I was pretty sure I heard a chortle or a snicker. Then she added, "No, *older* than dirt!" Her little voice definitely laughed over my curiosity and her helpful revelation of my spiritual path through past lives.

When I was 12 years old, the telltale sign of womanhood appeared. I remember heading outside, the screen door slamming behind me, and trying on womanhood for the first time. I declared to myself, to the trees, to the grass, and to the sky, *I am a woman!* I waited for a response or a change of feeling—something new to happen. Surely, this was momentous and I would feel different. *Ta-dah!* There was nothing. I shrugged and joined in the badminton game already underway in the yard.

Years of womanhood passed. One summer day amid a sweltering heat wave, Still Waters suggested I retreat from normal activities into nature. *Allow yourself to relax, flow, and be cleansed*, she seemed to say. A mental image came to me of a Native woman sitting on a soft mat of mossy rock in a creek, cool water laughing across the bed of stones. What relief the mental image created! I relied on it often in coping with womanhood.

Alas, talkative is not the hallmark of her purpose. Let us start with the well-known idiom: *Still waters run deep* meaning quiet people are very thoughtful. With Still Waters' guidance, I have opened to my depth and grown more reflective. I have magnificent meditations—energy, color, vision, past lives, insights—and shields.

She has walked with me through the discovery of my shields—shields of the four directions and heart, growth, and energy shields. We are moving together around the Native American medicine wheel of healing, expansion, and Spirit.

A shield is a circle, symbolizing the self, wholeness, the cycles of life, and the Earth and the Sun. Receiving a shield vision is a deep meditation and special experience of spiritual achievement.

Shields were common among Native American tribes of the flat, open plains, where protection in battle was not provided by rocks, cliffs, trees, and hills. Battle shields were made of hide, tough enough to ward off arrows. The symbols, ornaments, and colors of the shields identified the owner's personal power and connection to Spirit. These latter aspects were considered the real source of the shield's protection.

A variation of shields has existed in nearly every culture on Earth. While some museums I have visited display one or two shields in exhibits, they may have hundreds in the archives. On several occasions I have asked tribal teachers about shield making and they will not discuss it, I think, because shields are personal, private, and sacred. It seems that shields are protected from public view as sacred, wondrous works of art.

Once a shield is completed, meditating with it deepens the owner's connection to the power and wisdom conveyed through its symbols and design. It is an outward reflection of the owner's inner world.

My first shield was white with snow, ice, and a frozen waterfall and creek. George sat by his golden fire that provided the only color in the design. A small bird perched at the top of a hemlock tree. A big bear stood on the cliff with me gazing down at the scene—the beginning point for my healing. A second, smaller shield hung from this one. It had a gray background made of felt (representing

11

"feelings") and silver thread stitched to represent sleet pouring down on a girl. All that remained of her body was a head and limbs. The torso had burned in the fire of hurt and anger. My spiritual work was to untie the knots that held the shields together, heal the wounds of this child, melt the frozen landscape, and flow.

This shield set presents the connection between spiritual work and physical life. My path has been and still is, about living in my body, instead of dragging it around. Living through the body, instead of feeling trapped in it, and refining how I connect with physical life.

For me, the modern female body is a confusing, complex lesson—from head to toe—that I have had to figure out. Learning to love myself and take care of my body are reflections of spiritual growth. I have had to change from ignoring my own welfare to making decisions about new routines, boundaries, and habits of loving the body.

From the soapbox, I espouse that the female body requires a lot of energy: from nail care, cuticles, and polish; to hair coloring, cutting, and shaving; moisturizing lotion, sun screen, and lip balm; facial wash, toner, wrinkle serum, and moisturizer; the dilemma of make-up—which kind, how much, blah, blah, blah; flossing and brushing; fitness—walking, hiking, yoga, weightlifting, abs and crunches, sports; and the big one—eating wheat-free, drinking tea, no sodas, no coffee, no sugar, no corn syrup, and enough water. Exhausting! Who has time for all this female stuff? Then there is the dentist, the eye doctor, the gynecologist, and who knows what else as you age! Still Waters, save me! Make it easy! Please guide me to learn to make the right decisions and 'do no harm.' I am happy to report that my attitude has improved and there is even the occasional pedicure!

Still Waters has come forward to return us to the real subject at hand: "When Louise stepped onto her spiritual path, her heart was frozen. Understand she was not a cold person. She kept her sensitive, intuitive, compassionate heart behind a wall of ice for protection. She had suffered much and feared more pain would come. For the sacred river to run through her heart, we—her Guides—had to slowly melt the ice and teach her to surrender to love. She faced many fears to do this. She now walks the Earth with her shields balanced and her body strong. She is a lioness, a leader, and the world awaits her messages."

My shield work with Still Waters indeed has been healing, as this recent meditation celebrates:

The holiday to-do lists were done and it was time to exhale deeply and reflect. Feeling the urge to meditate, I was aware of a groundswell of support building for the moment. The fireplace roared with a hot fire for warmth on the cloudy, winter afternoon. Gentle music led me into a peaceful journey.

I closed my eyes, focused inward, and Bear, a Spirit Guide in the form of a bear, was waiting for me, as I had suspected. Bear lives in the west of the medicine wheel, represents feminine energy, and inward searching. "Follow me," he said as he turned and bounded away. I followed, asking, "Where are we going?" He called back to me, "Into the woods. You are starting a new cycle. You are a leader. Take the leader's chair. People need you."

I stopped in my tracks. Noting my fear, Bear said, "You are nervous because you don't believe in yourself."

"Believe in myself? Believe in what? What does it look like?" I asked. Bear showed me a glimpse of my crystalline white inner nature, and then took off.

I followed his big, furry, bounding rump into the woods. Ah, "into the woods," is that a metaphor, a simile, a symbol, or what in literature? In meditation speak, it means "into the heart." Going there with Bear, means seeking your future from the darkness to bring it to light.

We reached a clearing in the woods and stopped running. Over to the right was activity. I noticed that various beings were draping me with a garment. This was an important ceremony and resembled a bridal party assisting the bride with her gown and veil. The garment had a plain bodice that formed a large "V" in the front trimmed with fringe and beads. Layers of the garment were an earthy brown alternating with a rich blue. The beads sparkled and the fringe swayed. I asked Bear about the color scheme, "Why can't it be white?" Bear explained that when I pass over, I can wear white, but now my shaman's cloak is brown and blue. I acquiesced to his greater judgment and accepted my new gift.

The cloak finally arranged in order, the helpers disappeared and I walked across the opening in the woods to my left. As I stepped slowly, the garment undulated softly, moving like waves on the earth.

A large, boxy chair appeared in front of me. It was made of wood that was energetic. It did not actually move, but it seemed to pulse. The chair was compelling. I touched one arm, carved to curve and arch like a leg and paw of a mountain lion. The other arm, I noticed, was the other front leg and paw of the mountain lion.

Meditatively speaking, a mountain lion is a leader—someone who is willing to stand alone, express their voice, and respond to life with love. This wood throne belonged to a leader.

Slowly, I sat into the throne and waited. My mother appeared and laid her hands on mine in my lap. Bear explained she was returning to me something that had been taken away years before. I knew instantly, that it was poise—the comfort and ease with one's self inherent in poise. It has been 50 years, and now it is my time to shine. The gift was returned to me and she left as quickly as she had appeared.

I rested back and laid my arms upon the arms of the throne, and cupped the paws with my hands. The mountain lion paws meshed with my fingers and we became one. Suddenly, the chair sprang to life. Whoa! I ran further into the woods on all fours carried at a graceful, bounding gate. Suddenly, a sea of faces appeared ahead of me. A warm feeling of compassion and caring filled me, and a voice said, "The world is yours."

Still Waters' Teaching: Lay Your Sunshine and Joy on Everything

Over time, Still Waters has taught me to seek my true self in calm, deep, and silent reflection. To express the beauty I discover through my crafts of writing and shield making. To express the energy of my name, Laughing Waters, through these crafts and through feminine living—receptivity and creativity. It is Still Waters who whispered to me recently, "Lay your sunshine and joy on everything."

Spirit Guide Still Waters
Shield

3

Come Into Your Power
Spirit Guide Black Rain

Reach beyond the world you live in.
Reach higher to find your power.

Black Rain, an Arapaho medicine man, walks in spirit now as a Guide for me. He dwells in a high mountain forest of tall, straight lodge pole pine and spruce that gives way to sun-drenched meadows that are peaceful resting places for hikers. Along with other members of his Arapaho tribe, he energizes the area. A fish-filled rivulet curves from meadow to meadow along its way to the large lake below. He earned his medicine name many years ago. This is his story:

The future medicine man of the Arapaho people had been in training for his position ever since he could remember. It was the calling that echoed throughout his being. His abilities were, as yet, untested. The drought on his tribe's land was seemingly without end. Plants normally full and succulent crackled with the crispness of death. People, too, were starving and dying. Others were weak and vulnerable. All traditional methods of prayer, dance, and ceremony had failed to bring the rains. The people questioned the condition of their society and feared the future.

Fear had grown from an unspeakable prodding at the edges of

their minds to an undeniable burden etched across their faces and weighing on their shoulders. The trust they had in their rituals was shaken—replaced with doubt and fear. *Could the spirit of the people break? Surely they would all perish without water, without rain.*

The tribe faced an uncertain future, and the moment of reckoning was near. They turned to their young medicine man in training and placed their hopes in him. He quivered under the seriousness of his people's need. He grieved the death of his tribal family members, feared that more would die—it was up to him to stop the suffering.

Heavy hearted and chilled with self-doubt, he entered a dark ceremonial cave in the mountain overlooking the tribal land below and prepared for his test. Fully understanding the importance of his actions, he depended on his inner voice to guide and direct him. He cleansed and purified his mind and body by smudging the air with smoking herb bundles that he had gathered and prepared in times more plentiful. He thought of his teacher, who was among those who had passed, and called in his assistance.

After building a large fire of dried plant material, he prayerfully welcomed the energy of the Sky Beings; Four-legged and Two-legged Beings; and Winged, Crawling, and Plant beings. Thick smoke curled out of the cave's smoke hole, signaling his personal ceremony to the tribe below. He gave his fears to the flames, making room within his being for the sacred, creative power of the Universe to enter at his invitation. Where fear and pain had dwelled within him, pure energy of strength and power flowed. He became aware that he expanded beyond the boundaries of his physical body in full union with Spirit. The flow of energy caused him to sway and chant. After an indeterminate length of time, the Spirit of the young medicine man departed from his body. Its pure essence lifted from the top of his head, rose from the cave, and ascended to float in the sky as a white cloud.

He penetrated deeply into the sky in search of the place of power among the clouds. While merging his essence with the place of power, with all his heart, he spoke in his native tongue of the need of his people to receive the abundant gift of rain. He described their desire to live and survive on the Earth, their need for the conditions of Earth to welcome them in return, their want of good crops, and their willingness to live in service to the Sky Beings in return for the gift of life.

The man-cloud reached the end of his prayer. He hung in silence, aware that he had no more to say. His heart's message was fully given. Stillness was all around him. "What else could I do?" he questioned. He waited for a response. He just waited. Then he saw it. The smoke that had carried his pain and fear appeared and rose in spirals before him. It gathered force and began to spin and form a huge thunderhead cloud—spun of fear and pain and suffering. The dark cloud seemed to be showing itself to him, making sure he understood. The two clouds faced each other, staring. A flash of blinding light emanated from beyond the thunderhead and carried him back to his cave and into his body.

Returning to his physical body and senses, he stretched in small movements to reconnect fully with the ground. He felt the hard cave floor beneath him, saw the cave walls surrounding him, and smelled singed embers and ash—remains of the fire, indicating that much time had passed since his ceremony began.

He closed his eyes again reliving his ceremony. "Was I successful?" he asked. He heard no rain outside the cave, but recalling the thundercloud, felt sure in his heart that Great Spirit had acknowledged his prayer. He thought about the purity of his being, his ability to travel from his body, his heartfelt commitment to his people, and his willingness to test his personal power. As he reflected on these magnificent aspects of his ceremony, the medicine man felt energy rising inside him and forming a mound of mastery built on a base of desire and aspiration. He sat at the top of the mountain and drew strength from the experience.

He realized that when the rain did come, it would be Great Spirit who answered his prayer—not the young medicine man—who brought the rain. He was the messenger of his people, and that was his purpose and his power. He realized that giving up his fears and embracing his power would encourage Great Spirit's response.

As he sat in the cave, in his mind he envisioned his desire: rain coating the mountain rock, teepee skins, and flesh of his people. Rain hitting the dusty earth, slowly at first, kicking up small clouds of dirt, and then dropping so close and so fast that the drops merge and cover the dry ground. With the rain, smiles grow on the faces of the people who emerge from their teepees and reach their faces and both arms to the sky. A new rivulet laughing and gurgling around rocks in the low-lying gulch, after having had no flow for months. The rain, causing the rocks to sing. The roots of the crops that could be revived swelling with the drink they so long needed. Water rising up in the plants above the surface of the earth and into the fruit. The drink bringing with it earthy nourishing richness. He envisioned this and he saw the faces of his people turn to him as their hearts filled with love and respect for their new medicine man.

He heard a voice near him in the cave bestow his medicine name—Black Rain. In his mind he heard Great Spirit say, *Use your power wisely for the good of your people.* Surging with relief, the young Black Rain gave thanks to Great Spirit and emerged from the dark cave to witness thunderheads gathering from the west.

Black Rain's experience of testing himself, giving up his fear, and asking for assistance from Great Spirit to save his people is the way to take power in life. From trust and faith, inner strength, self-knowing, and power grow. This is what I must do. This is the focus of our relationship.

Black Rain has come forward to say "Like me, Louise's power lies with water. She is learning this connection, and to pray for her family's safety and for her own safety around water, to pray for the welfare of humanity around water shortages and catastrophes, and from a higher perspective, to bless the springs, rivulets, streams, lakes, rivers, and oceans—sending love and peaceful energy around the planet. This power is needed on the planet as the scales of balance between humanity and nature tip.

The Indian Ocean Tsunami of 2004 in Indonesia, Hurricane Katrina in the southern United States, the Pacific Ocean Tsunami of 2011 in Japan, and other events call her to pray.

Earth is the water planet where humans live. Humans use the planet to master their lessons relating especially to emotions—the inner waters. We Guides work with Louise to calm her waters and teach her the beauty of a peaceful life."

I have learned that he has known me in many lifetimes—we have been married and known each other in every sense of the word. As my Spirit Guide, he provides power and protection to me and my family. Black Rain watches over us and offers direction. He makes sure that my life experiences are orchestrated to bring the proper tests at the proper times. He loves me with the totality of his being. His existence is dedicated to my mastery of soul lessons—particularly related to stepping through the hoops of fear that diminish my fulfillment. I revere his role and am in awe of his dedication.

I first encountered Black Rain, meditatively, walking the land of the Arapaho people. When he came forth and introduced himself to me, he stood strong with power bundles and a staff near a Rocky Mountain lake. He pointed proudly in the direction of the people's water supply. When he departed, he turned his back to show me his sinuous body bare to the light, gleaming and radiating the essence of his power. The magnetism of his energy was breathtaking. His strong shoulders were draped with a beaded belt that told the history of time. His left arm lifted to the sky, encouraging me to reach beyond the world I lived in, to reach higher and deeper. This single, sure motion and his strength and power let me know to trust my path, but the vision of him left me in confusion. *Reach for what?* I wondered. *What am I reaching for?*

GEORGE: Ah, confusion! Confusion is one of the greatest teaching tools. When humans become confused, they are at the brink of a new understanding or new experience. This is true whether they are studying algebra, entering their first real love relationship, being fired unexpectedly from a job, mourning the loss of a close relative or pet, or opening to new spiritual understanding. It is known by all the Spirit Guides that humans fling themselves into a tailspin at the first moment of confusion.

These times of confusion are fertile plains for new growth, self-discovery, and new creations. The mind starts to ask new questions. The heart desires resolution from the discomfort of the unknown. The spirit either soars with the prospect of exploring new territory or retreats to hide until the feeling of safety returns. The lessons people need to master regarding the physical body and being in it are encoded in their cells.

Each of you decides with God what you will tackle in each lifetime. At birth, you pass through a veil of consciousness into the physical world, where much of Spirit life remains hidden from the mind. But rest assured, everyone is here for a purpose; and when you reach inside beyond the confusion and fears and pain of past experiences, you can discover your personal truth, your power, and the full abilities that you bring to this world.

Some of you are here to serve the whole of mankind. Some of you are here to resolve your own personal issues that remain incomplete from past lifetimes. If you treated someone poorly in a past lifetime, you may be feeling their response to that event in this lifetime. If you seem to be suffering unduly in this lifetime, take a look at your need to grow stronger. Allow your confusion to be your teacher.

Black Rain's Teaching: Go Through The Hoops of Fear

Black Rain provides warrior protection to my family. He covers us like an umbrella. Over time I have learned to feel the love that is bestowed upon us. He has led me to attain a higher perspective of living and dying and of suffering and freedom, and to see that love exists all around me—all the time. It flows to me and through me out to the world.

While George focuses on melting and disassembling my protecting wall of ice blocks, Black Rain encourages me to strengthen my inner core and step fully into the flow. "Go through the hoops of fear that challenge you," he says, "not over or around them. Go through them. And for you, the hoops are on fire." *Oh, great!*

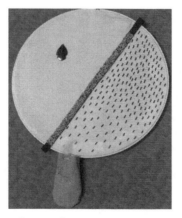

Spirit Guide Black Rain
Shield

4

Our Charge, Louise

GEORGE: So, here we are—Still Waters, Black Rain, and George—working together with our charge, Louise, helping her unlock the doors that have closed over time, rediscover hidden treasures, trust the power, fly free, and serve mankind. She is like a treasure chest waiting to be opened.

Since she likes the wilderness, let's sit together in a place she would like, as I share her story. Say, by a gently flowing stream of laughing waters in a hemlock forest. Sit on a log close to my snapping fire. Warm yourself in the bright glow of my fire. Never mind the falling snow and blowing wind. Let the coldness of life fall away in front of the dancing flame. From here, understanding and truth flow.

Her birth name this lifetime is Louise. Her Native American name is Laughing Waters. Yes, you can say she is older than dirt, having lived here many times. She has learned about herself and the experience of living and dying. Her soul is wise, although her lifestyle is not limited to the robes and rigors of a religious temple or the traditions of a holy person. She lives freely an ordinary life—in an extraordinary way. She wakes up each day with wisdom of the ages and lives among you wearing her Merrells®, heels, flats, Birkenstocks®, moccasins, skates, and snowshoes.

When she was 27 years old, the cycles of time were right for the spiritual lessons to accelerate. Many seeds had been sown. The actors were on their marks. Earth was deep into its final dark phase before reaching the end of the millennium. It was time to prepare this young teacher for her role in the spiritual growth of the civilization. It was time to unlock the memories that were keys to her own healing and enlightenment, so she could share them with the world in this book.

For her, the path inward to enlightenment was through the heart. It was time for her path to cross with one particular soul who had as his purpose the role of supporting her in this lifetime. His name is Jim. If they met and chose to have a relationship, we could begin to help her unlock the secrets of her spiritual life through that relationship. Because of their past histories together in numerous lifetimes, the chemistry between them would be great, we knew, but would they choose commitment to a long marriage? It might require some effort on our part! On a number of occasions, we whispered in their ears, *this is the relationship for a lifetime.*

They did marry! The walk down the aisle was a walk into the unknown for both of them. They were fearful, but each of them had recognized a special quality in the other that they could not resist.

The experience of living with a husband, blending her habits and expectations in daily life with a partner, was new to Louise. Actually, it is probably accurate to say that she had never been really close to anyone before. It was a perfect relationship for opening her heart. There were ups and downs. Her frustration with his aloof behavior grew. She felt there was a pervasive lack of support coming from him, and she could not create a feeling of *us* with him. Not so ironic, his life lesson is learning to create harmony; hers is a lesson of learning to feel.

Over this one frustration, she learned to truly feel and express the anger that burned inside her. This anger was either going to kill her or lead her to healing. By activating the anger, there was hope for activating healing. Louise wondered why Jim's behavior (in her interpretation of it) was not true to the love they shared. Their love, she sensed, was bigger than both of them.

A vague image developed and came to her repeatedly when she argued with him. She could see large, shiny knives clanking together, with enough clarity that she would even check the kitchen drawers for knives. She had no reason to think that her partner would use a knife in the rage of the moment, but the vision of knives clanking together was attached to the emotion. Interestingly, the rage was inside her, not him, but she projected it on him.

Even after they moved to their first house and life seemed to take on new meaning, confrontations continued and so did the knife visions. Her husband would bring home new purchases for the household—often with a little guidance from us—like knives or utensils for the kitchen. This fed the fire. Louise's mental images became even clearer over time.

Soon, their son, Matt, was born. This experience, more than any other, proved the ultimate stimulus for clearing her heart. Motherhood awakened the depths of love and fear and protection needed for good soul searching. It also provided another avenue through which new friends and experiences would enter her life. Up to this point, everything had been introductory. The real soul work was about to begin. She and her husband were intended to be blissfully happy together. There was a way for her to have this joy.

The mother of a friend of Matt's invited her to a reading with *a psychic who works in the Light*. These carefully chosen words actually meant nothing to her, but did pique her interest. The other mother, who was young and playful, contrasting with Louise's more serious nature, issued invitations for fun activities. Our charge had never been to a psychic reading before, and we saw to it that nothing got in her way of attending. A great opportunity awaited her. She arrived punctually and in time to hear the end of the reading for another woman.

When it was my turn, I sat across from the psychic, Sara, and had a vague image of a scene in my mind, similar to the knives, but different. Suddenly, I repeated several times with great vehemence to Sara, "I *hate* water lapping on a dock." Not, "Hello, nice to meet you," but "I *hate* water lapping on a dock." Sara softly taught me to, "Never say *hate*. The energy sent out with that word into the Universe will come back around to you."

Huh? I had just received a great lesson in higher wisdom, which I comprehended, but sticking with my now even clearer vision of lapping water, replied, "I *really, really don't like* water lapping on a dock." The calm, understanding response from Sara was, "Of course you don't." Sara, a very powerful woman, could blend her energy with mine to see the emotionally charged memory.

I later learned that a typical psychic reading focuses on someone's future events and decisions relating to money, friends, employment, and so on. Sara and I went right for the deep stuff—stuff from the past.

Confusing stuff! *What is going on here?* I wondered. *I've never thought this before. What am I seeing? What are we talking about? I'm talking about something that I have no idea what I'm talking about!* My

28

mind was clicking to comprehend what was happening, where this conversation was going, or where it was coming from.

GEORGE: She was asking questions—hooray!—the key to higher learning. This was the beginning of The Golden Door opening. New levels of awareness, memory, and power could emerge from Louise's heart. Will she stop here? Leave the reading in rage or continue on? This was a big moment. Briefly, she felt tricked, sensing her mind was about to be reorganized. Louise has everything neatly packed and stored away inside closed compartments. She does not like to feel tricked. Will she reject this opportunity and close down?

Sara, whom we had carefully chosen for her gentleness and great capabilities, was equally challenged. She recognized that Louise was being indoctrinated out of the blue and had not studied or read about any of this *psychic stuff*. Sara saw Louise's gray aura covered with dark holes and surrounded by question marks. The aura of a person is an emanation of energy around the body that indicates fears, wounds, and disease in the body, as well as how closed or open and flowing the person is. A healthy aura has the colors of the rainbow.

The psychic reader wondered if she would be able to read Louise, or whether she *should* read her because of the degree to which Louise appeared to be lost. As soon as the reading continued, they discovered the value of these visual images.

Sara explained that we were seeing a past life. *A what?* She continued, providing some details. "You had been a young, beautiful girl kidnapped by pirates. They treated you poorly," the psychic said. I saw the fierce look in Sara's eyes, sensed the anger rising in her, and knew this was an understatement. I fleetingly noticed that I could feel what was inside her. Our energy fields had blended—one of the skills of powerful medicine, I learned. We clicked.

Who is this psychic, Sara? We seem to have stepped out of time into our own creation. Our souls connected, not our minds or personalities, but our souls. She is short and her hair is white and long, wrapped beautifully on her head. She sat very still and did not seem to see with her earthly eyes, but with her mind's eye. There was no pretense. I sensed gentle power and purity and responded to her willingly.

We sat together silently while traces of the experience surfaced in me and ran like a movie with textures, faces, smells, sounds, and vague emotions. It had been a slow, painful stripping of dignity, sanity, and breath. Indeed, the memory of water lapping on a dock *was* a painful memory! I still carried the emotion of it centuries later.

On two occasions prior to the psychic reading, I had awakened from a dream where I was drowning—choking and gasping for breath. Especially because it was a recurring dream from childhood, I wondered about its significance. With this new knowledge of the pirate lifetime, I thought it was time to get my drowned, dead self out of the water and back to shore!

GEORGE: We Guides agree! We want to see all the broken pieces of our charge's Spirit healed. If she ever had a quick, life-expanding experience, this was it! She was through the Door and ready to keep going. We cheered her on. We could see she was intrigued and drawn to learn more in a quest for relief from fear and suffering.

My attention jumped to the knives. "What's with the knives?" I asked Sara. "I keep seeing and hearing clinking, clanking knives."

"Jim had many lives as a warrior," Sara replied. "It's not knives, you hear. It is swords. You're connecting with his warrior nature and a past life you shared."

My turn with Sara was up and the reading ended. I knew that life was more complex than I had previously comprehended, that there *was* more to life than meets the eye, and there is history: I actually live time after time. I connect with these events, places, faces, and emotions and am sensitive to these memories. My weaknesses, fears, and challenges are scars of unhealed wounds from unresolved past lifetimes. I have to rediscover these events and make peace with them to achieve wholeness.

GEORGE: Louise had received the clues and direction she needed to answer her questions and solve her mysteries. This work, though, was up to her.

Louise's Medicine Bag

31

PART II
JOURNEYING THROUGH PAST LIVES

5

Love Never Dies!

As I moved forward on this spiritual journey, my meditation skills developed and my intuitive abilities heightened. These had lain just beneath the surface, ready to come forth when I needed them. The spiritual life is not far, light-years of travel away. It is right here with us, nearby, within reach. The reaching is our responsibility.

Sara revisited me on several occasions in the ensuing years. It was under her guidance that I had my first two shield meditations. After the first one, I said to her, "Oh, Sara, this is so neat. We should do this together with other people!" She gave me her, *Ah, me* look that meant I was missing the point. I focused and heard her tell me that this was my work—for me to do alone. It is my gift. *Oh, I have a gift!*

One day while meditating with a group of women, she handed me a message she had received from my Guides and written down. This message was:

> "You have had a fantastic growth year! Your Guides are filled with joy to have you aware and searching. There are so many directions for you to search. You are standing in the middle of the Light. There is a circle around you with many doors. Which one to choose? Just choose one. The others will still be waiting. Each door contains a new, exciting mystery. Open and enjoy. Study, enjoy new friends of the Light, and grow. Great Spirit's love flows through you to others and back to you. Your life is to be happy this time around. Lose those

fears or recognize that they have no power over you. Dance in the Light!"

It felt like a school report card, and I realized I was not alone and that I *was* in a classroom—a school for spiritual growth. Which door did I go through? Which classroom? The doorway to past lives. I searched for the lives that would quell my intense emotions and bring me peace.

The clinking, clanking swords revealed themselves first. In meditation, I journeyed back to the great Coliseum in Rome during the time of the Roman Empire.

✳

I see that the time is ancient Rome, a dusty, smoky place located not far from the sea. Rome is a mecca, receiving people from all directions. This day, people come for the Games in the iconic, colonnaded arena, the Coliseum. Outside, the noisy crowd moves around—gesturing, yelling, and greeting one another. There is rivalry and drunken celebration in the air. From bottom to top, the arena fills with the hierarchy of society—regal senators and nobles in the best seats up to the simply wealthy and then the poor, the women, and slaves at the top. Colorful standards at the pinnacle wave in the breeze. Holding areas for the condemned, the gladiators, and the beasts are below.

I think the custom of enjoying the spectacle of death is peculiar, but the Romans revere it as entertainment. Slaves are trained as gladiators and pitted against one another until death as entertainment or to celebrate a holiday. Many wear weighty shields, helmets, and leg guards and use long, heavy daggers and tridents as weapons. The whim of the crowd decides which defeated gladiators die. Based on their cheers, a defeated gladiator is killed or allowed to live depending on the empathy he has evoked—and on the mood of the crowd.

I find myself there in the arena on a small stage above the granular sandy floor. I am not a gladiator, but a young slave woman/actor in a show before the Games begin. I sense the familiar comfort of being there with my partner in the present lifetime. Yes, he is to my left on the stage, a fellow actor and we are doing a scene. Our stage is surrounded by the tiers of the arena, layer upon layer. I look out to the faces all around us, watching us. How many faces? 10,000, 20,000, 30,000, 40,000, maybe more. They wear the flowing fabric of togas and garb accented by colors and regalia of their rank and honor.

My costume is a white stola, flowing from one shoulder to the ground. Accenting my shape is a shiny gold braid wrapped across the chest and waist. I feel beautiful, almost dreamy in this pure drape. I wield my lightweight weapon, a lancea, ineffectively against my opponent with humor in mockery of a fight. Although we are not real gladiators, it is important to please the crowd. Laughter and some jeers reach my ears and we continue the animated charade. The crowd is noisy. My partner is wooing me and I fend him off with my weapon. We are both slaves, deeply in love and unable to marry because of strict rules of class structure. Our love is visibly electric, sparked by the taboo.

We are entertaining, joyous, and flowing with fun. I feel good— lighthearted and happy. All is well, and then suddenly, the mood of the crowd changes.

Jeers rumble in the lower circles of the crowd as if to say, "Enough of this innocent gaiety! Give us bloody thrills." My stomach tenses and my movements cease. I stiffen. The crowd's energy builds to a frenzy and spreads like a contagion up through the surrounding rings of faces. The men rise from their seats and stand in protest to the theatrics. They wave their arms in bored, drunken displeasure, calling noisily for a kill. Their raised arms are showing thumbs down! There has to be a kill. A kill! Comedy becomes drama, becomes tragedy.

Pandemonium is all around me. Panic is inside me. One of us has to die. The throng is a deafening noise, threatening, overwhelming. Fear is paralyzing my body and making my mind blurry. *Ego annegamus! I can't kill him!* This I know. *I cannot kill him!* But one of us has to die. My chest is heaving with hard breathing. *I am tricked! Trapped! Angry!* I cannot catch my breath. I am confused, lost, and weak with panic. In a moment our eyes meet—his and mine—and our souls agree: I will give my life this time; he will support me in another lifetime. This is the way it will be. This must be.

And it is done. He moves behind me where I cannot see him. Wrapping his left arm close around my neck, he pulls me against his torso. My lover holds me close in this warm, strong embrace. Our bodies touch in familiar places. The crowd loves this seductive killing. His mouth near my right ear whispers his love to me. My lover holds me—*may this moment never end.* I close my eyes against the nasty crowd and the sight of my love's right arm rising above me with dagger in hand.

(Here, now recalling this event, I withdraw from the memory, unable to face it. An ache develops above my right breast and a red mark appears on the skin, foretelling the place where the fatal stroke is thrust. This memory emerges from the depths of my body and mind, riding an emotional river of pain, betrayal, and humiliation that washes over me.)

Returning to the memory, I am struck by my lover's dagger. The unthinkable happens. Fear and confusion become pain and shock. These feelings swirl with more fear, hate, and anger. *What did I do to deserve this?* I am overwhelmed with grief, with rage, and with pain. *Why did I have to agree to such a thing? Why is it this way?* The noise of the crowd is fading. *I can see them, but can't hear them so well now. I HATE them. THEY did this to me. Lethum ad tu, Imperator! Death to you, emperor!*

It is hard to remain alert. My senses fade in and out. Hatred—my last thoughts are vengeance for the crowd and the murder. No one was supposed to die during this play acting.

Pain and anguish make me sensitive to each microsecond of the suffering, and it seems to take a long time for death to come. Such suffering! *It takes a long time.* I struggle with the pain.

Finally, I am rescued, swirling out of the pain, out of the body clad in white. At the hand of death and the moment of passing, I fill with agony, grief, self-pity, and longing for revenge. *Nobody cared about me or my body. I was tricked and used.*

"Look," I say angrily to the attending angels around me, "They have just tossed my limp body on a hard, wood cart and wrapped my arms across my chest."

The angels watch with me. Indeed a lone servant pulls the cart. During the bumpy ride out of the arena, my body rocks and my left arm falls from my chest and flops over the edge, hanging toward the ground, lifeless, and bumping good-bye to the riotous crowd.

My defeated corpse, cheered by thousands, was valued no more than the life it had carried! The blood left behind on the arena floor is *my blood*, simply erased with new layers of sand. Separate and stunned, I grieve for myself in my own ironic tragedy. This society says I am a slave, of no value, useless, worthless. *"I am not!"* I protest.

✳

I understand that we have known each other before, Jim and I. Yes, this is true. Suddenly, many things I had noticed in life started to make sense. What relief!

Profound things, like the way I felt when I first met him. We were in a group of people at a large round table in a Chinese restaurant on a Sunday evening. We were all participants in the same seminar on a dinner break. Each one introduced him or herself as they chose seats. There were two women to my right and next to them was a man. As I said my name, our eyes met, he said his name, and my heart sprang out of the center of my chest, seemingly three feet in front of me. I felt like I had been struck deeply, and I could not really hear or see. My senses blurred. Something between us connected. Something flashed.

While this was an intangible experience, it was so vivid that everyone at the table felt it, especially the woman next to him who was provoked to firmly warn me, "He's with me." I immediately withdrew into denial that anything had just happened, sat down, and buried my face behind the book-size menu. After six or seven months, during which we had numerous encounters on the sidewalks of Washington, D.C., at lunch time, and at parties, we finally decided to go on a date.

Other things made sense, too, such as my intrigue with the Roman Coliseum during art history class in college. At that time, I did not know why I was fascinated with it—the magnificent structure ingeniously engineered and designed for horrendous acts of sacrifice.

I am very uncomfortable in large crowds and never take center stage. I experience panic, loss of breath, and pounding heart! This response to being in the spotlight has been something completely beyond my ability to control or resolve, and this, alone, has had a profoundly sad impact on my full participation and enjoyment of this lifetime. It is so strong a force that it cripples and scares me, rising up to be healed.

Jim's warrior attitude in the relationship had been if I get what I want, then he does not get what he wants, and vice versa. One of us has to lose every time. Whether we are planning something as simple as a day's activities or how to spend the next years of our lives, he acted as though we could not both be happy at the same time. Obviously, this set up conflicts with my philosophy of seeking unity and harmony in the relationship.

If each of these truths were a piece of something greater, what was the something greater? What is the whole truth? These were my questions that opened more doors!

The Healing

The shock, pain, and scars of this Roman lifetime left wounds on my psyche now ready for healing. Resolution of my concern over knives came pretty quickly for me—paring knife, carving knife, bread knife, chopping knife, butter knife, all have quieted their cacophony. Their metallic echo was successful in stimulating the spiritual warrior in me.

Stage fright remained a haunting issue, as did trusting my husband. I meditated to revisit my dramatic actor's death at the fickle turn of fate in the Roman Coliseum to gather more insights to aid these deeper healings.

✱

Floating above the arena with a bird's eye view of the passionate crowd surrounding the drama, I discover something of great importance that I had missed at my actual time of death when I was lost in a haze of passion:

I see I am wrong to think that no one cares about me. My partner has fallen on his knees next to my body. He is weeping. His hands cover his face. He is weeping for me. His love lives on, and I can feel it. He loves me in death. His love is unaltered and transcends death. Down there he is weeping. Up here, I witness little hearts and lights floating from his heart to mine delivered on the smile and wings of a small, round cherub! Such comfort!

This is overwhelming. It is such relief. My body surrendered to death and I am rewarded with this vision of love—love that is fuller, richer, clearer, purer than I could ever have imagined. It is so awesome, it is beyond comprehension, but it is real and I can feel it.

My Earthly body is gone, but our love remains. The life of Shardra, the slave, is not a waste! I receive the love he sends me and send my love back down to him to heal this pain between us and unblock the flow of love. We are one, in love.

✳

After this enlightening meditation, I see as separate from myself, the lurking, threatening shadow of fear that had remained with me. The clanking knives, battles, stage fright, trickery, audiences and crowds, and the hand of fate. They are stepping stones to my understanding the indestructible power of love. We live and die as individuals, but our love lives forever.

In that lifetime, I experienced the violent, ignorant, and frivolous lark of mankind in creating and victimizing slaves. I have wept and agonized for my own pain and for all slaves whose blood soaks the earth. However strong and aggressive the plight of mankind, it cannot harm the love that each soul creates and carries or the ability each has to heal from the pain and suffering of physical life. I know this now.

The bigger picture that this Roman tragedy illuminates offers me the power to decide it is safe to return to the stage of life to play my role. With this new wisdom and healing of love, I am more powerful than any threat. *Fear, I say to you, put on your black hat and cape and walk out the door! I need you no more!*

No matter what occurs in life, our love cannot be destroyed. *Amor immortalis!* Love never dies.

This year, 2011, Jim and I celebrated our 30th wedding anniversary. With clarity of our relationship ever increasing for me over the years, I am touched by his selflessness, dependability, dedication, and loyalty. These qualities underscore the small moments of day-to-day living with him.

He has said to me many times, "You are the center of my life." I feel his love for me as the great gift that it is, and love does flow freely between us.

George's Interlude

Louise has bravely relived the experience of an unexpected and violent death and public humiliation. This process of releasing the past is the path of her healing. It requires her to learn about herself, develop an expansive view of who she is, and achieve healing by passing through hoops of fear—much like the young Black Rain.

Yes, Dear One, there is something bigger going on. Oh, those clinking, clanking daggers! What mysteries they uncovered! We, her Guides, are pleased to witness her relief. She is a Blessed One and is ready to live a loving, joyous, peaceful life.

As she continued to exercise her newfound ability to bring up the past, she uncovered another powerful memory of unexpected death and humiliation. This time, the humiliation was self-imposed.

ॐ

6

Forgive Yourself!

In a brief moment of relaxation one Christmas holiday, I sat on the living room couch, closed my eyes, and, in a visual meditation, saw Still Waters retrieving a battle spear from atop the front range of the Rocky Mountains. She descended from the mountains, floated across the flat plains, and confronted me nose to nose. With a deep look, she handed me the spear, smiled, and slid away. However, when the spear reached me, it had changed! It was a staff with a ball of light on top.

End of vision and beginning of more confusion. I thought it must be a sacred gift since it involved a ball of light and the Christmas holiday. *What did that look on Still Waters' face mean? She changed a battle spear to a spiritual staff. Hmmm.*

> GEORGE: We love to stretch the skills of our charge. We know she will figure it out. She keeps reaching (thanks to Black Rain's encouragement), and we keep feeding her hunger to understand and to resolve. She has never before seen a staff with a light on top, and she is wondering about that light and what Still Waters' smile meant.

Eventually, I recall my association with the staff. I envision a warrior spirit alternately sit by his fire and pace around the rocky ledge, enraged. His energy and male voice come up from deep inside me eager to be recognized and heard:

45

✳

When I was many moons younger, I was a great Chaticks-si-Chaticks Warrior. Chaticks-si-Chaticks means Men of Men. You call us the Pawnee. Strong, proud, and fierce. Respected by the village, I am Thundering Bull, their protector. I had many children. I warmed their mothers' beds and lived in many lodges, providing food for them all from the great buffalo hunts.

The Chaticks-si-Chaticks lived in the wide open space between the long water from the north and the high mountains that block the sky, where the corn grew tall and the buffalo ran free. This was our land. Even our enemies—the Sioux and Cheyenne—honored this land as Chaticks-si-Chaticks land. My people lived there for many, many years before my own grandfather's time. The buffalo were gifts to the Chaticks-si-Chaticks from the Great Star Nation above.

From my youngest days, I learned the ways of the warrior. There were tests of skill and courage and speed. I did well in these, so that my people would be protected. My success, cheered by my village, covered them with peace, like the big, starry sky above.

My heart remains weeping for the last time I rode. I weep for the plains, for the land that was ours, for the village unprotected, for my children, and my brothers' children. Tricked by the enemy. I sit here, stuck—old and white-haired now—by my log fire atop the first range above the land that was ours. For many years I watch over the land that lives in my heart. Water runs down the high mountains through the canyon to reach the land where my village lived. It flows like tears, but cannot wash the blood and the memory that was left on the land. It cannot raise my bones left there with a bullet in the right side of my head. Soil—good for the corn, good for the grass—soaked with Red blood. I weep for my people, I weep for the land. I curse the White man and banish myself.

I readied myself for battle that day, the same as always. Moving through the village I say good-bye to my family and give them love. I take myself, alone, for ceremony and battle preparations. In my mind

I pray to the Great Spirit. With my voice, I chant to him over and over while dancing freely with myself:

Ho He Ho
Ana Nana He

I surrendered my strong, solid body and became something greater. The right side of my face painted with two slashing red lines on the cheek and a red circle around the eye. The left side painted white. I marked my body with a red circle on the right leg above the knee for Great Spirit and told him: I am the one. Send here your protection and I give myself to you fully.

Clothed and painted and decorated for battle—fearless upon my horse—all fears released by battle preparations. My medicine, my shield, my spear, and bow and quiver filled with protection from the big star sky above. The village was in my heart. The power was in my hands. Determination was in my ride. My mount beneath me, I rode—a Chaticks-si-Chaticks Warrior—at one with the Great Spirit.

I led my warring party in a line to the ridge. The enemy line appeared over the sunrise ridge ahead. We rode in attack. The horses fast, feet pounding. The wind blew hard against our bodies and carried our battle cries—sacred sounds that called in Great Spirit's protection. I was an eagle flying over my body and horse. I welcomed the enemy. I embraced them. I wanted them. We closed in to fight.

Suddenly, great noise! Explosions! My body was down. Around my stricken, trampled body are legs of horses and confusion in the clouds of dust kicked up. I saw my foe—a familiar Sioux face. Rifle in hand. Cries of victory filled the air as the enemy annihilated my warring party. We lay prone and lifeless amidst the squealing, wounded ponies. I was lost in the cloud. Death took me! White man's weapon—guns! I watched my defeated body and mount, and my broken battle shield fallen in the dust.

The enemy rode on, armed traitors, to finish their victory. Complete death to my village. My wives, my children, my brothers, all.

I died willingly, but the pain remains in my heart. My hand still holds the useless spear. I rage with anger. I have seen these guns on the belts and in the hands of the settlers marching across the land. These are not tools of the Red way. These are cowardly tools needing no skill, no bravery, nor talent.

My Spirit rose up to the ridge. I raised my spear and screamed a battle cry to every star in the sky and every man on the land: *This is my land! Give it back to me! Give me back to it!*

My angry, bitter rage turns to weeping. I remain by my fire, tricked and saddened, a fallen, foolish warrior. I watch the Great Plains land, the land that belongs to my people. The land I lost. I watch the changes on the land. Time moves. I stay stuck. I am mad at myself for being tricked. I banish myself for losing the land of my people. I refuse to forgive myself—so many died. I keep myself in shame, separate from Great Spirit, a torturous existence with a crushing feeling of wrongness and anger in my head. I reject Great Spirit and hide from his embrace.

I watch Pawnee people living in another place now. I will NOT put out the fire that burns for the land of the Chaticks-si-Chaticks— for the blood of the Chaticks-si-Chaticks villagers, warriors, and broken battle shields.

✳

The Healing

The warrior's anguish is my anguish. His shame is my shame. I must set him free. This legendary tribal story keeps me in shame and isolated from life. The taking of Pawnee life and land paved the way for new settlers through strategic trickery. My anger at being killed so artlessly and effortlessly is a scab on the surface of my ego. Under this scab, the wound seethes and festers with intense guilt and shame for my failure.

Still Waters retrieved Thundering Bull's staff and handed me a staff of light, a scepter, many years ago, and only now, as I connect with Thundering Bull and his story, does the meaning of her smile occur to me. It is time to make peace, and I thank her for giving me the opening and power to heal this memory.

Only now, do I understand the transformation of war spear to spiritual staff; of anger to passion; failure to power; self-inflicted anger and shame to self-forgiveness; and the transformation of my being in releasing the past from my tight grip.

I see Thundering Bull on the cliff with arm outstretched reaching toward a star, setting himself free from Earthly bondage and returning to the hands of Great Spirit—Tiakarwa.

Now I carry the scepter of a great warrior. I walk the land with the staff of a Chaticks-si-Chaticks warrior, with love for the people and protection from above. His warrior spirit beats in my heart.

The weeping and raging can end. Self-forgiveness can come. I open to acceptance by Great Spirit and welcome that union. The battle for peaceful existence is over.

Now I walk the land with the staff of a great Chaticks-si-Chaticks warrior, with the staff of a great Chaticks-si-Chaticks warrior. *Ho!*

George's Interlude

Our charge is getting very good at resolving confusion and healing herself. Her warrior spirit and connection with the land remain strong, but she alone cannot change the progression of humanity on Earth. This she learned.

We got her attention a second time, while she was on her living room couch for a trek to the other side of the world—the next leg of her journey …

☙❧

7

Listen to the Animals!

WHILE RELAXING AT HOME ON the couch one afternoon, my attention was drawn to the back of a dining room chair. The grain pattern of the long slat of wood moved into the shape of a lion's head. Startled and disbelieving, I looked away and focused my eyesight on another object. Returning my attention to the chair back, I again saw the lion. It faded out and faded in. I looked away several more times, yet I still saw the lion in the grain of the wood of the dining room chair! Then I could not see it. It was gone.

I started talking to myself and paced around the room. *How did that happen? What did it mean? What was that? Can you believe it?* While it was there, I struggled with accepting it and failed to connect with it to find out why it was there. When it was gone, I struggled with losing it and wanted it back. I calmed myself and sat in silence. The answer came: A past life on the African continent, an area now divided into Kenya and Tanzania.

✳

I recall the lowland palm trees and the clear, calm Indian Ocean; the deeper, darker forests and the large crystal clear lake farther inland (source of the great long river); the free, open plains dotted with acacia trees and wallows carpeted with red oat grass, sweet star grass, and the tall guinea grass; and the lofty, snow-capped mountain rising above all. These are the homes of the animals I know and love. The herds of giraffe, wildebeest, and elephants that migrate with the seasons; the lone rhinoceroses that remain in the savanna through the dry season; elegant, swift cats cleverly camouflaged in the dappled shade and tall, yellow grasses. Browsing, grazing, stalking, swarming, living, and communicating according to their natures. It was my home, too. I lived joyously in the trees and brush with my animal friends—wild and free from the rules and structure of humans!

From just above, I can see an opening in the forest, drawn in by the sound of beating drums—hollowed out tree trunks stretched with zebra skins. The activity there cuts through the peace of the natural world. There is a gathering of dark-skinned people, wrapped with cloth and painted. The soil is dark and moist—it must be the rainy season. I see a person held captive by the tribe and feel tense, trapped, and angry. I am the captive! This tribe is dangerous for me. They practice witchcraft. They make special drums and keep bees. They are preparing to kill me this night for living free with the animals. Enraged and unwilling to experience the physical suffering of beheading, I escape my man body and the earthbound world and seek refuge with the animals watching from beyond the tree cover.

We all look down on the scene together—animals, insects, and me. The leader raises his strong, impassioned arms and with one movement, takes his deadly swipe—in the opening in the forest. I drift away higher, glimpsing the mountain, the plains, the forest, the ocean. The elephants and cats in their homeland places knew. The rhinos and gazelles knew. The humans, who could not hear the animals talk, did not want the one who could, to live. *I do not understand this. What is wrong with the way I live, wild and free among the animals? Man is evil. I am right to live as I did, with the peaceful animals.*

*

The Healing

After learning of this past lifetime, I very unexpectedly re-united with the tribe's leader whose hand had brought the deadly blow.

On a hot August afternoon, Jim, Matt, and I attended an enjoyable gathering of healers held in a Japanese garden. The garden had herbs and meditation and eating areas. A bridge arched over a pond with fish, lilies, and lotus blossoms. It was a wonderful setting for a wonderful time. I had eaten and talked, and eaten and talked some more, and the afternoon was fading. Feeling rather complete with the party, we contemplated leaving to go to our next commitment that day when a new group of people arrived.

I caught sight of a short, round little elf-like woman entering the garden with an entire entourage. Her energy announced: stand back, give me room, give me lots of room, do not approach, and take it slow. She sat several people away from me at a round table under an umbrella. We did not speak directly to one another, but the sparks flew as we observed each other.

Being August, the bees were ubiquitous. Most of the healers present were successful at communicating with them and keeping them at a distance. I, on the other hand, was like Pooh Bear's honey pot.

I wore a particularly long pair of dangling earrings, which I had not worn before or since then. A large, menacing bee would not give up! He just had to get involved with my right earring. It did not take long before he got down to business and stung me. Although he stung me on the lower neck, my pain occurred in three places below the shoulder.

Naturally, the newest Reiki student at the gathering was selected to practice his technique and heal the sting. He did okay, but the bee toxin was still in me. So the little, round, elf-like lady with the stand-back-give-me-room energy, who had been watching closely, stood up and came over to me. She bent over to begin her method of healing.

I looked deep into her eyes. And I knew! Energy coursed through my body. My mind reeled with the closeness of this woman, who had been the man with the execution sword centuries before. *She was the one! She was there! She did it! Arrest her!*

I could see the scene again in my mind's eye. In a low, cool voice trying to cover the rage rising beneath the surface, I said, "I know you."

The woman did not respond, and I repeated, "I know you." Silence. I continued: "We were in Africa together. I was a man. I lived with the animals. I was killed."

Her wise, slow response: "And with this day, our wounds are healed and the past is behind us."

What! I screamed in my mind. I am exploding with rage and am not letting go so quickly! I bemoaned my needless death. *She knew! How dare she impose her will on me!*

The healer said, "You were a man who lived against the rules of the tribe, so you were beheaded. The power you had was considered evil."

Argh! I am seething and trying to be gracious in front of the gathered healers. *How does she get away with cutting me off at the neck and then thinking healing a simple bee sting makes up for that? She has been wrong for centuries and I walk around angry for centuries because I have been wronged...oh, God, not more forgiveness ... oh, no!*

On the other hand she didn't have to heal the bee sting. She could have ignored it. She did eliminate all traces of it right there. She did share her power with me. Maybe forgiveness is justified. After all, it is my heart that heals with forgiveness, so they say.

Oh, brother! If I keep thinking like this, I won't have anyone to be mad at. And I'm mad! And I'm right! Couldn't she at least have to say she's sorry and display some indication of having suffered from the guilt of her judgmental action?

I decide I have had enough of this party and depart with Jim and Matt.

GEORGE: Here it is again! The lesson for Louise over and over on this Earth is dealing with pain and anger and lack of freedom. She gets angry at the way her life is taken. She gets angry at the way her energy or dignity is taken. She gets angry when she cannot be heard.

The Healing

The events of the Japanese garden party months ago inspire me to contemplate their purpose. I think of Africa, my Africa. A 21st century impression of Africa might include civil strife, disease, hunger, and oppression—a place where the people are a people of need. But I am aware of an earlier association with Africa—the home of the great wildlife on the planet. I recall the lion that reached out to me in the wood of the dining room chair a few years ago. A vision of lion returns now, leading me to the savannas and forests and reminding me of what is important. I discover it is good to hear and feel lion's voice again. It has been a long time since I could hear it. It has a soothing resonance and brings peace and warm satisfaction all the way down to my gut, where it vibrates within me.

Lion's voice rumbles:

"Embrace the animal kingdom. Watch us. Know that the behavior we display for you is a lesson. Learn from us. We are not here to be dominated by man, but to teach you. Learn from us.

When our lands shrink too much and we are gone, where on the land will humankind find this teaching? We are here for you now. We remain here for you still. We are older than you and carry the secrets of survival and living and dying. It is our full-time job to display this wisdom to you. We mirror these secrets to you. Whether we are the lion or the lamb, we bring peace. We ask not to be tamed, but to be heard.

Hear the herd messages. Migrate with the elephant herds and follow the rhinoceroses; fly with the vultures; swim with the turtles. We, your peaceful teachers, all have lessons for you—survival, living, dying.

Know that every time you look at us, we are looking back at you. We know your nature. We know when you are open and listening and what you desire.

Louise, lioness, like all your sisters and brothers, teach the civilizations of every continent the secrets. Let peace be your way and Oneness the source of your roar and your purr. Run free with me in the Light of the bright golden sun across the grassy plains through the consciousness of the great lesson that is Africa. Walk like the mighty cat you are—with silent strength, determination, and courage in each step; with patience and experience in your pace; and with your purpose gleaming in your eyes. When night falls, roar under the moon and join with others of your kind. Remember the rhythms and heartbeats of life in the wild.

Once, the land was free. There was lots of space for all of us. Changes came. My mother was killed by hunters. "Who will feed me, protect me, and teach me the ways of the pride?" I cried out, lost and sad. I would have perished but for another lioness whose heart opened to me. She taught me to adapt—for we are both the hunter and the prey. I learned the pride's territorial boundaries, how to react to danger, when to fight and when to surrender, and proper customs of behavior. Learn from my story that the lioness is the heart of the pride, teachers of propriety—yes, propriety—for survival in these times of change. Mothers are important!"

Then the other animals have their say.

Elephant continues with his guidance:

"Like the lion, we protect and teach our newborn dutifully. The cows and calves live as a herd with the cows nursing, teaching, and caring for the calves. The bulls, like me, live alone or in pairs. We communicate to each other in low frequency sounds, audible by us miles away. We know who is in the neighborhood and what is going on without newspapers or CNN® television.

As the largest and heaviest land mammal alive today, I am unique. With a large head, my memory is extensive. My ancestors lived 50 million years ago. If man were less interested in hunting my kind and taking the land where we live, we could be a most successful species. Alas, man considers man to be the most successful species.

All throughout our lives, we never stop growing. I am magnificent, engineered for balance and strength. My legs like columns, my backbone like an arch of steel.

Louise, have you heard my message? Understand your body. Know how to use each part, especially that which is unique to you. Check your structure for strength and balance. Feel your skin—what kind of protection does it provide you? Play like a child no matter what your body condition is—go roll in the mud! And never stop growing. Learn, experiment, test yourself until the end.

What do you remember of the ages of your existence? Move with the elephant herd across the plains and enter the unknown of the dreamtime. We will meet you there and together dream your existences."

Rhinoceros snorts:

"You look at me and think I am odd and silly. Now I say to you, it is I who is laughing at you. So serious and critical and judgmental, you are! If I looked differently, I would not survive as I do. I am strong and powerful and fast. My thick, tough skin allows me to go through prickly places that others cannot. My skin is my armor and I have lots of it. So what is the matter with a little sagging skin? My behavior is threatening and that, too, is my protection. I love my mud baths and my two horns. I can uproot a tree and find my meal in nearly any condition. Enough time with this. Do you understand me? Shield yourself for protection and seek nourishment! Snort! Snort! Snort!"

Giraffe observes:

"You have a very unusual voice this time, Louise. Learn to protect your uniqueness for it is the seat of your power. Unwise humans cannot tolerate what they cannot themselves understand. 'Differences' matter to these people and they do not live with honor and respect for those that are different. Know your predator as the ignorant human.

Swing freely through the jungles, forests, savannas, and hills of the land. Live fully in your own unique way, but open your eyes to those that threaten you. It is not the dark jungle evening or the insects or hungry wildlife that threaten. It is the ignorance of humans. This is true here in Africa. This is true in America. This is universally true.

Do not stop being who you are, and focus on improving your perception of those that are different. See your predators for what they are capable of doing. They are hungry—hungry for control and revenge.

Do not be afraid to stick your neck up. Reach for the higher perspective. Your neck is gorgeous. It connects the mental part of you with the heart part of you. Let the voice it carries be heard. Golden messages from above walk the Earth in you. Stand tall. Stand proud. Be different, like me. When words fail you, think of me. Rub my soft neck with your warm human hands. Let the words rise within you. I am here to help you this way. Lots a' neck for lots a' words!

I have missed you these years. I call for you and finally you can hear me again. Be smart this time. I love you, Elegant One, and connect you to the whole through voice and laughter.

You know I see a lot from up here. I look down on everyone. Many discount me because my head seems lost in the treetops; however, it is a higher perspective I have.

Just as the neck connects your head part with your heart part, your long legs connect you to the earth. Nothin' wrong with skinny legs and knobby knees! I have four. Others who were envious of you tried to take yours. Reach for those long legs again—think of me to do it. Eat green. Express yourself. Use your legs. Be elegant. I live in you."

Zebra bellows:

"Let my stripes hypnotize you. Climb onto my back and ride me into the void where nothingness embraces all of creation. Dip into the darkness and return to the Light cleansed and jewel-like with a stronger, clearer understanding of transitions, movements, and change. I am more than a superficial optical illusion! Experience the secrets of living and dying with open-mindedness and a willingness to explore unknown territory.

Experience deeply—see, feel, hear, learn, know what is over the edge. Become more and more familiar with *alternative* aspects of your consciousness, so that your awareness expands, broadens, deepens, and becomes ever fuller. There you will discover aspects of yourself that have remained hidden. This is your future unfolding to you. Reach for your vision."

Insects buzz:

"Welcome to the land where human life is old and animal life is even older.

Insects
Small.
Crawling, Hopping, Flying,
Chirping, Beating, Singing,
Making music in the dry and dark land.
Beetle. Termite. Locust.
Mosquito, Fly, and Ant.
Bottom of the food chain.
A powerful domain.

We dart through the landscape spreading the news, giving warnings, sharing the animal world with the plant world, water world, and wind world. We support the smaller beings that support the larger beings. We are the base of the pyramid with all other mammal, fish, and bird life above.

Why do humans think they have so much to learn from each other—more than from Nature around them? When the wooded savannas, forests, and rain forests of the world are being used properly, the natural balance of insect life and life dependent on insect life can be maintained. Imbalance at its worst will mean the insects will live alone on the Earth with the Sun, the Moon, water, and plants. This is a possibility!

When you see us, really look at us. Listen to us. We have much news to share. Today we alight on your consciousness to teach you that even though we are small, we are not unimportant and not nearly as unintelligent as you think. All living things carry the vibration of intelligence and a voice of communication. All creation has the same right to life. Are you surrounded by flies? Crawling with ants? Pestered by beetles or crickets or water bugs? Sharpen your listening skills—we are talking to you!"

The green energies remind me:

"The plant world provided your home in Africa. The rain forest was your habitat, your sustenance, your playground. All who lived there were your friends. As plants we teach personal qualities. Some bite and are poisonous. These plants remind you to be careful and gentle with others of creation. Some are tall and strong and provide shelter. These are like your best friends, husbands, wives, relatives, or parents under whose wings you are safe to grow.

Just as humans are spirits in a physical body with heavenly guardians and angels attending to you, each plant is in-dwelt with a Spirit and has a Guardian Spirit or Diva. Living as a lone human in the wilderness, you lived in connection with the Spirits of plants and animals—in peaceful harmony and interdependence, which you continue to seek on Earth. The plants grew from the physical balance of nutrients, water, and light, and the plants blossomed and flourished on the spiritual vibration that echoed throughout the forest."

My anger over the beheading and need for revenge dissolved among these true, heartfelt voices of Nature. These connections are what I lost and what I need. Lion does not visit through the chair now. He pulses within me. His energy runs through me like the waters in a swollen riverbed late in the rainy season. I am full and this past is healed.

With closed eyes I see my own Spirit body with a large dark hole on one side. Green energy moves toward it. The circle of the hole opens to the green, healing energy and fills to become one with the greater whole. My Spirit form reappears in profile and a large mass of green energy moves along the heart and throat, opening the pathway between the heart and the voice that had been silenced. How lucky I am that the little woman came to the garden party—and that she came to me in love.

I am given back my voice to express what is in my heart. I am given back courage and closeness to the Earth to walk the land in honor of my purpose.

Sijambo (I am fine), my animal friends!
Karibuni (Welcome) and asante (thank you)!
Harambee and hakuna matata!
(Let's pull together. There are no problems.)
Ha, ha!

Reflecting on insect's message, I wonder, *can I hear the insects now? Do I understand?* Spider stands out. I fear spiders and have had numerous encounters with them. Spiders find me. Anywhere, anytime I can run into a spider. My most peaceful encounter was on an early morning hike in a primeval forest of western Maryland after a snowfall. The sun was up and casting shadows, as well as glistening on the many spider webs that decorated the trees. I wondered about this—*is this a rarity to see spider webs in winter?*—and a high, squeaky female voice replied, *we like to come out and enjoy the morning after a storm, too.* This was a magical moment.

In what I consider an initiation into the spider sisterhood while on vacation, I was bitten during the night on the back of the neck by a brown recluse spider. The venom that can kill a person attacks the vital organs and shuts down body functions. The skin can continue to be eaten at the wound site and require skin graft transplants. The doctor took me to his office to show me on the Internet what to expect before releasing me with my prescription antibiotics.

I did not sleep more than an hour each night for the following week. I started losing weight. When I returned home and went for my regularly scheduled acupuncture appointment, I summarized my life for the last month and almost forgot to mention the bite. I added the brown recluse bite to what had occurred, and my acupuncturist whirled into action. He admonished me to seek treatment as soon as possible after a spider bite or snake bite. *Who said anything about a snake bite? Oh, no, does that mean I have another initiation waiting me?*

Acupuncture is an effective antidote for toxic bites, it turns out. After one treatment, I was able to sleep, and after the second treatment, all signs of the toxin were gone. The wound healed completely.

Spiders, symbols of infinite creativity, represent female energy and, in some lore, are said to have spun the alphabet to develop communications. Spiders are writers and weavers, telling the stories of time, like my finding the universal value in the stories I have lived. Condor was right: a Spider Woman me!

George's Interlude

Louise is learning to accommodate her experiences from beyond the veil of consciousness into the life she is living on Earth. She is learning her truth; healing on the emotional, mental, and physical levels; and creating a spiritual life. We are pleased with her progress and growth. Serious spiritual work and healing are good, but it is time for her to discover a life of joy, where she lived simply and danced and spun barefoot—her feet upon the earth.

৯৩ ৫৪

8

Find Your Joy Song

*

I<small>N MY ADOBE ABODE</small>, I spin and dance to a song of joy. Baskets woven of grasses sit on the floor—others stacked high up toward the ceiling. Baskets used as trays and bowls for gathering, cooking, storage, and sifting. Woven of stiff grasses in spiraling coils and decorated with geometric designs in red, green, or yellow. My heart beat merges with the drum beat of the Earth and my inner song consumes me in a hypnotic trance:

The earth is dry
Beneath my feet,
Protects me in my
Mesa dwelling.

Sky beings above,
Ancestors below.
Ladders, kivas,
Sipapu. Peace.

I rise with the sun
And face the east.
Drumbeat in my feet
Echoing through my being,

Heartbeat of the Earth.
We are The Hopi.
Visionaries
In the dusty, dry land.
With every step
We praise the Earth.
My feet on the Earth,
The earth on me.

Drumbeat in my feet,
Echoing through my hands,
Heartbeat of the Earth.
Basket Maker
Is my name.

Reeds and grasses
Through my fingers,
Rainbow colors
Wrapping, bending,
Curving, swirling.
Round and round
Like the Earth
Beneath my feet.
Basket Dancer
Is my name.

Twirling, bending,
Swirling in the
Circles of the Earth.
Weaving joyous
Colors in the
Baskets of the
Dusty, dry land.

Drumbeat in my feet,
Echoing in my mind,
Heartbeat of the Earth.
Dust upon my feet,
Soles upon the Earth,
Hopi Woman,
Basket Maker,
Basket Dancer,
Am I!

✳

This memory has swept through me like a gentle tornado and taken me out of body. I awaken and lift my head off the computer where it dropped as I wrote the song.

Where did I go? I went to learn that the stars are in charge of Earth. The Earth is not the source of the joy. The Earth is a boiling place ruled by the stars. Hopi are from Earth in body and from the stars at heart. The Hopi know the secrets of the truly peaceful heart. It is not something they learn, it is who they are. *Hopitu Shinumu* (the peaceful ones) living on the cracked, dusty land under turquoise blue skies. They are here, still, like the animals, to teach this way to those who want to learn. As sky beings in the physical body, the Hopi live simply and purely, with little need for possessions.

Hopi teach the value of prayer and ceremony, resourcefulness and creativity, and the music of joyous living. As survivors, the Hopi remain undefeated—living quietly so the music can play for them, in them, and through them. The Hopi know rhythms of the seasons, rhythms of Earth, and rhythms of the rise and fall of civilizations.

If you are looking for a role model, shed your modern ideas and look to the Hopi. I entreat you to feel their pulsing heart and find the higher wisdom.

Do you see you are like the basket? Woven of the Earth, an empty vessel for filling with a song of wisdom. In a simple basket, do you

71

see more than grasses? Do you perceive more than emptiness? Can your Spirit flow into the basket and hear its song?

> <u>GEORGE</u>: Our charge has journeyed back to her Hopi lifetime to recapture the experience of joy. In this simple and sacred lifetime, she introduced color into the basket making of the Hopi people. It is the reason for her love of baskets in the present lifetime and is her connection with the southwest United States and its deserts. Her Earth connection and spiraling work with the plants and plant and mineral dyes was her expression of joy.

This past life does not require healing. To the contrary, it gives me energy. The beauty, clarity, simplicity, and creativity of the Hopitu Shinumu inspire me. My Hopi connection deepened with a dream:

As I settled into bed one night and had just closed my eyes, entering a world between physical reality and dreamtime, a vision began with three little Jeeps® driving in from the left with their headlights on. The vehicles turned toward me. Their lights shone in my eyes and were blindingly bright. Suddenly, the lights exploded in a flash and three Kachinas appeared, dancing. *The Kachinas are visiting me and dancing! I am being visited by the ancestors!* The most visible one is all black with white fur at his wrists and ankles. He is jolly, clown-like, showing off his fur. He is a joker. Another is deep red, almost maroon. The third is more difficult to distinguish, even though I strain to define his appearance. They dance like puppets or court jesters, happy and lighthearted; and I return to a dream state of lightheartedness, Kachinas, and my adobe dwelling.

The Kachinas have transported me back to my Hopi lifetime, where I see that my baskets are the flow of the Universe. Each has its own song and dance. I, too, move in rhythm with the heart (drum) beat of the Earth. Dust upon my soles. Joy in an untarnished existence.

I can hear my Guides chanting rhythmically, "Keep dancing and express your unique movement. Embody the joyous flow. Joy is in the body."

Still Waters encourages me to continue my circular dance in shield making, and I reflect on weaving: the single strand of fine thread that makes up the web of life, connecting us all in a Universal fabric. Oh, the joy of being with the Kachina Spirit dancers!

George's Interlude

Louise has lived many lives in the wild, or out in the elements, as you might say. Hardly ever has she found the joy of life indoors. Don't misunderstand me. She's lived in palaces filled with ornateness and conveniences, servants and royalty. These things brought pleasure, but not joy. She found her joy in the simple desert life of a dancing Hopi basket maker—with the dust of earth upon her feet.

Remember Louise's first memory that surfaced when she sat with Sara, the psychic reader? It was Louise's hatred for water lapping on a dock. This is a very painful experience and we have waited for the right time for her to uncover its ocean of fear and outrage. Where did her playful, dancing feet take her? Let's see what learning lies beneath her dockside memory.

ॐ ଓ

9

I Am Not My Body!

<u>GEORGE</u>: We whisper to our charge right before dawn one morning, *when did you stop jumping in puddles?* She stirs and awakens to the new day wondering, *when did I stop jumping in puddles?* The thought crosses her mind on and off all day. She does not know where this question will take her, but we guide her.

My TRAIN OF THOUGHT BEGINS with the most recent memories of Matt tramping through puddles, concluding that there are many ways to jump in puddles. He would jump with both feet creating a big splash. Or he would shuffle through one foot at a time making small tidal waves. Or he might carefully approach near enough to keep his feet dry, and then edge in closer ever so slowly, keeping the shoes just at the edge, then move a little closer, then closer yet, breaking the edge and walking into the water. He playfully experimented with the puddle. I smile at these memories and think, *yes, there are many ways to jump in puddles. Many ways to get the feet wet ... to get in the swim of things ... to dare to experience ... to live spontaneously ... to feel life. When did I stop living this way? When did my feet stop moving?*

I remember my ballet and tap lessons. My feet moved then. The Mexican Hat Dance, the Can-Can. Plié, pique. Plié, pique. Shuffle, ball, stomp. Shuffle, ball, stomp. I recall my mother saying, "Miss Joyce says she is disappointed you are quitting her dance class. She says you're a natural, very talented." I have no response for her. I'm quitting dance. I'm seven and a half years old, almost eight, and I'm done with dance. Why am I quitting dance? What made me decide that? I enjoy it and feel good dancing, but I'm making this decision to avoid something. I don't want to make a mistake and feel shame. I want to hide.

GEORGE: She recalls a family weekend in Annapolis, the historic waterfront capital of Maryland, a few years later, when she was maybe ten years old. The buildings were made of brick. The streets were paved with bricks with puddles here and there. The dock was rough-hewn timbers. Standing at the edge of the wharf, looking at the murky water slapping against the edge, she felt chained, restrained, and frozen with fear. The sickening sight of water lapping on a dock. This is one of the most emotionally charged connections she can make. She had made a mistake—a *big* mistake with consequences. Her life did not have to go this way, but her innocence, lightheartedness, and puddle-hopping took her where we could not rescue her. Louise is ready and recalls her colonial New England seaport life when she was a young girl of eight years old.

✱

I really don't like water lapping on a dock. Why?

Mother, who appears to be the same mother I have in this current lifetime, is hanging laundry outside under the big elm tree. The long sleeves of her cotton-print dress are pushed up tight to the elbow. It is a hard life with hard work and mundane routines. We are both lonely. The home she maintains is a one-and-a-half-story stone house that appears to be cold, dark, and empty. I see no light in the windows or doorways. It feels like a place to be from, but not a place of potential for the future. There is an absence of pleasure; life is a routine of drudgery, except for reading books at night by the oil lamp. Books stimulate my imagination and encourage me to dream of other places.

Outside in the yard, which slants toward the street, I can smell the ocean on the breeze. I am humming and dancing around under the big blue sky, free-spirited. My chores are done for this afternoon. I feel so beautiful in my favorite dress. I like the sash tied at my waist and the nice bow at the back. I know it is not as good as some girls have, but this one of mine is my favorite. "Emily Ann, don't wander past Main Street," Mother yells to me. "I won't, Mother," is my automatic reply. But I do go past Main Street. I head to the docks, where the big ships anchor. It is exciting with activity.

The wind coming off the water whispers of the faraway places it has been as I playfully match my footsteps to the bricks and planks. The breeze calls to the wild part of me to wander and explore. *Surely there is more excitement in the world than in this port*, I think, *than on these brick streets or in these brick buildings. Across the ocean are older places with riches and treasures and royalty—kings, queens, and princes! Some people think that this place is "it," but I think this is a good place to be from. I'm going out beyond the horizon, someday, beyond what I see here.*

I have wandered to the puddled, brick-lined docks where I really do not belong. It is dirty and smelly. I know I should get home. These dirty old ships with dirty men. I turn to run back and run right into the big, strong grip of an overpowering man. Two others laugh at me. He stops me by the arms and holds me too tight, laughing with bad breath and rough beard and bad teeth. His eyes are dark. All three of them are ugly. "Where are you going?" they taunt.

Where am I going? I suck in my breath in shock and cannot find a way to breathe out. The more I try to fight loose, the more his grip hurts. *I'm going home*, I think, but the words won't come out. "Let me go. *Stop!*" I scream. A dirty, coarse hand muffles my screams. *It appears I'm going with them.* What is going on? Dizziness. Dragging my legs. My beautiful dress. He is dragging me onto the ship. Stench. Filth.

Others like him circle around like the predators of the sea, sneering and hungry. He releases his hold on my arms and I stumble backwards against the wide, dark, rough-hewn planks of the ship. I can't get back to shore. I'm like a caged bird. My arms hurt from being grabbed and dragged. My throat hurts from screaming. I am shaking with anger and fright. He's laughing at me insanely. He is an animal. He is not civilized at all, but he is in control.

An opening leads down one level where food is prepared and eaten by the pirates at long tables, which are also made of wide, dark, rough-hewn boards. I am put to work here. The galleon sets sail. *I won't be home tonight, Mother. Maybe they will dock the ship here again tomorrow.*

Sickening. Everything is sickening. The movement of the ship on the ocean. The look of these men. The smell of these men. The unknown. The roughness—the boards, the beards, the skin, the habits, the language, the sea. I should not be here. I am a target. They watch me. They touch me. They have control of me. They laugh at me. I wonder what I do to make them behave this way. I don't understand this. I had prayed to God to sail the ocean and see the other lands, but this is not what I asked for. I don't belong here. How could He do this to me? I am Emily Ann.

I am on the ship for a long, long time. I call to Mother in my head. I send my love to her and ask the wind to carry my message to her. I want her to know where I am. I want her to find me and rescue me. It might be a long time before she sees me ... The cold, hard, heavy shackles that I wear much of the time have worn open wounds on my wrists. I am dirty and smelly. My clothes are unrecognizable for what they were. I fear I am not the same either and will never recover my life.

I cook their food. I serve their food. That's all I do willingly. I eat the food to stay alive. I don't talk to them. I don't speak at all. I don't give them one word. I pretend they can't hurt me if I don't respond to them. I can't stop thinking and that keeps me going. I think and strategize on the inside, but, obstinately for protection, I don't let it show. Sometimes I can't help but scream when too many of them take me at once on the tables where they eat. They gather round. They line up and hurt me. I scream until I pass out.

Time has passed. Blood oozes from the sores that have appeared on my body. I am nearly useless to them now. I am having trouble thinking. I feel like I am gone, as if into the fog that hangs on the sea, and then I return from somewhere unknown. These men are bad. I am good. I should not be here. I cannot figure this out. I used to think about slicing them dead with my cutting tools. It would feel so good to stop the dirty laughter and watch their blood run. I am too confused now to even think about that.

The water goes forever. There are no ports. There is no hope. I am too weak to stand. It must be the painful, oozing sores doing this to me. The men whip me to stand, to work. They press dung on my face. I think I have lost my mind … I am not afraid … I am not anything … I am not who I was … I am not who I was going to be … I am someone else.

I lay slumped on the galley floor all the time now. Shackled on the hard, rough-hewn floor and staring into the cracks, crevices, and knotholes in the wood. This disease is eating my body. Hatred consumes me. I am attracting flies and am useless. I'm so lonely. My mind is gone. They stand over me, kick me, and sneer.

I see Mother. I can see her face. She is smiling and calling to me. *Emily Ann! Emily Ann!* The breeze gently moves through her hair and across her face like the fresh laundry snapping on her line. She is soft and beautiful and warm. *I love her so much. I'm coming, Mother. I'm coming. I'm coming home.* Indeed, I am dizzy, spinning into a bright Light.

Several of the strong men, who are familiar to me in this current lifetime, drag my chained body up from the floor and lug me, limp, up the ladder into the cold air. Strong wind hits me. I pass through the gusting wind and sink into the cold graveyard. Water is above me, below me, all around. I can't breathe. I can't get out. Choking. Choking. Choking. Then just blackness.

I release from the dead body and heavy shackles. I release from the body! *Oh, what relief! No more struggling. I am free again. I have no pain. I am free. I can breathe. I can float. I can move. I feel no pain. I live on. I am all white. I am separate from that painful body. Oh, joy! I didn't know this. I didn't know. My body is dead, but I am not. I am not my body. I AM NOT MY BODY! AH! I AM NOT MY BODY!*

✱

<u>George</u>: It is with great courage that Louise reviews the harshness of this past suffering. She has unmasked the source of anger and fear that closes her heart and the experience that her body is a place of pain and suffering. Her old rage suffocates what fear has not already left paralyzed. She is able to release the anger, pain, and fear, and rescue her spontaneous, curious, wanderlust from the cold ocean waters. She can now develop fortitude to stay centered in her body when life gets *rough*.

Our message to her is to find her land legs; forgive the pirates whom she knows again in this lifetime; forgive herself for the mistake she made as a carefree, puddle-jumping girl; and continue her happy dance across time in pursuit of her dream. Follow your imagination, Dear One, for it *will* unlock the gold inside you.

The Healing

My tears flow, and flow, and flow for innocence lost. Death was better than life. In death the suffering ended and the discovery of my true self occurred. I am more than my body. I *have* a body, an Earthly self, and I *am* Spirit.

I have to forgive teasing, disrespect, bullying, nastiness, usury, rape, and reminders of the filthy, rough pirate life. I cannot even find the words to describe what I endured. These written words will have to suffice. As giraffe warned, the ignorant human is the real enemy.

My heart aches to be home. Take me home. *I'm home, Mother!* Where clean, white sheets hang on the clothesline, whipping in the breeze. Where a mother issues her protective warning. Home, to a predictable life and simple chores await me. Where a loving heart aches to hold me and empty arms are filled. Wrap the crisp, fresh sheets on my bed and let me lie upon their softness and forever be at peace.

This memory has sat heavily on my body and I realize I was coping with it all the time unknowingly. With healing came a release of the connection to the energy of struggling and suffering. I felt it go. It moved out of me and away. I have been harboring the memory that was sapping me of joy—holding it down in deep, dark waters like a monster that hides and feeds at the bottom of the lake. All the while, it was eating me like a cancer, sucking my joy.

Be nice, my father advised me recently from the other side. I defended myself in protest, *I am nice. I am the nicest person around!*

He clarified, *be nice to yourself.*

Oh, I realized, *he does make a good point. There are some changes I could make there. I matter, also. I do matter. I am worthy.*

It is my responsibility, as it is every individual's responsibility, to manage and nurture my own energy. I need to replace old habits of overeating, nervous eating, and critical harshness with calmness, honor, weight loss, confidence, openness, and pleasure—out of love for myself.

Fear, I'll tell you again, I have no use for you anymore. Put on your black hat and cape and head out the door. *Get out!* I need you no more.

George's Interlude

Our Readers, Dear One, everyone, refrain from abusive habits. This is what Louise's father means by *be nice to yourself.* Replace the energy holding negative memories with a new flow of energy that reverses and releases the negativity. Then feel your worth and beauty. Let all of your beauty radiate out. It is your protection. You are safe.

Our Dear One has lived many lives, including several as a holy person in various cultures over the ages—Kahuna and Buddhist monk included. During this lifetime as Louise, we have rewarded her progress and encouraged her growth with special friends. These relationships foster a quickening of experiences, camaraderie, learning, and fun and laughter. This next story is about Louise and such a friend.

ॐ

10

Lighten Up!

✻

I AM DRAWN INTO A NATIVE American village by smoke curls that rise from the center openings in the lodges then blend into the foggy sky above. The village is quiet, knowing it will soon lose its eldest holy leader. She outlived everyone her age and will soon join them on the other side.

I observe my own passing from my lifetime as Chisa (*Cheez-ah*), the tribe's holy person, with the assistance of my closest friend, the medicine woman, Talking Bird.

Deep in Chisa's cloudy eyes, the void is already visible. Lying on her softly cushioned mat, she breathes heavily and with great effort. The teepee fire burns hot for the comfort of the dying one. Talking Bird smudges and chants over the wrinkled, weak body.

To smudge, she burns a mixture of sage and other herbs in a bowl that waft a constant flow of smoke into the air. Dried sage keeps away negative influences and helps Chisa connect with the spiritual realm.

With strong hands, Talking Bird pulses the energy above and around the frail body, with hands rotating through the air automatically knowing what is needed. Her eyes gently close, she exhales, and her inner darkness gives way to inner vision as her mind replays moments of their lifetime together.

"Together we created magic. We carried the love and wisdom

needed to steer our tribe through good and bad times," Talking Bird said aloud to her friend. "No matter what the tribe was forced to endure, we combined our Spirit medicine and Earth medicine to heal the wounds of heart and flesh and to lead tribe members through confusion, suffering, and even death."

Talking Bird continued to recite honorable thoughts on Chisa's behalf. "We led lives of purity—never marrying or enjoying the strength of a good man. Our powers were considered so valuable to the welfare of the tribe that the sharing of our energy was protected by tribal custom and saved for the good of the whole community. While our physical lives were separated from normal life, our teachings permeated every moment of tribal life. We lived right. It is a job done well."

How else could a peaceful tribe survive and thrive in these threatening times? As children, tribe members mastered lessons regarding peaceful living. They learned of the power of Spirit and to invite Spirit into their personal power centers each day. The tribe lived with abundance, joy, and satisfaction, connected to the energized land of the deep boulder canyons, the rolling hills, high in the peaks, and down the running mountain streams, all under the glorious, broad, blue sky.

Smiling with the memory of their fun, Talking Bird observed, "It has been some time since we ran together in the rock canyon that was *our place*. Our feet carried us deftly, nearly flying across the rocks and boulders of dark granite into the deeper, darker places of the canyon. We acted like children there. I can even hear the familiar sounds of water rushing over stones and the scent of hemlock branches softly catching the wind. We retreated there together, often, to run and laugh and dance away the seriousness of our responsibilities and gain new energy, returning to the settlement calm and centered again."

A canyon is an opening in Earth's surface. It is a doorway into Earth, the medicine woman smiled with the memory of their teaching this to the children. "The energy between us was strong, yet soft, dynamic and peaceful, electric and loving—like the force of two magnets attracting, or fleas to a dog!"

Sounds in the teepee halt Talking Bird's reflections. Opening her eyes, she sees that Chisa is sometimes conscious of her body and sometimes not.

Without her partner, the energy they shared will diminish. Talking Bird, alone, will finish turning over the power to the younger medicine person. Then it will be her time to pass, too. Talking Bird lamented, "Chisa, you never were patient. You never did stay by a campfire once it faded. You wouldn't stay at a feast once you had eaten. Now that your work is done and the next holy person is ready, I guess I don't expect you to remain with me."

Chisa is with us—her Guides and Angels, Talking Bird heard a voice say. *We are here to help her let go of the Earthly plane and ascend to Spirit. We are here to remind her of who she is and where she is going—to help her choose to let go of her Earthly identity that is weighing her down.*

Taking this cue from the Guides, Talking Bird lovingly pulses her hands faster to activate more energy for her friend. It takes a lot of energy for the soul to leave the body peacefully. She knows this well. The holy woman is comfortable. Her breath will stop at the moment she chooses. A peaceful passing is the gradual loss of senses through which Earthly life is experienced—sound, smell, taste, sight, and touch.

Talking Bird recalls the vision she had the previous night of a lone white Spirit horse standing expectantly on a hillside pawing the earth, looking around and nibbling on grass, waiting, waiting for his rider to be ready for her journey. Two nights before Talking Bird had had a vision of the white wind moving with great force through Chisa's dwelling. It stripped the dwelling of earthly objects and left in their place pure white snow and space. All was being purified and readied for passage. Earth connection was clearing away.

Chisa's eyes fall open. Talking Bird completes the circular motion of her hands over the body, fully clearing away the spirit-body connection and freeing her friend to the world of Spirit to float and drift, to be ubiquitous and to play.

Briefly, Talking Bird releases the energy of their soul relationship. She feels it lift from her heart and go with the friend as she hums and chants the tribal prayer of death and passage.

Talking Bird knows that the holy one will soon be looking over her. She will feel Chisa over her shoulder. And she will hear her voice guiding her and giving direction—and opinions of which there had never been a lack—from the omniscient perspective she will have. For a while, Chisa will remain close. This is the way of the soul. And in their canyon, Talking Bird will call to Chisa and Chisa will come.

Surrounded by her sacred bundles, prayer feathers, trinkets, and beads, Chisa's effort to let go is done. The village gives her up. Talking Bird's heart is lifted by a vision of her friend's smiling ascent.

Chisa had longed to embrace the Light again and yearned for the reassurance of the Spirit world. Only now does she begin to open and become aware of Great Spirit's words. She realizes she is in a place of unending truth and love—back in the heart of the Light, and it feels good.

So, here I am in the Spirit world. Been gone a long time. Have to get used to being Spirit again. No more heavy body to carry around. Hrmmpf. Need rest. Old and tired. Worn out. No good energy left. Need rest.

Spirit's liquid-warm voice inquires: How are you feeling, Chisa?

Chisa: What do you care? I'm old and grumpy. Now leave me alone. I want to be left alone.

Spirit: Why?

Chisa: No rest down there. It's hot and heavy and tiring. My body hurt, the fun was gone.

Spirit: Why?

Chisa: Why? Do you know what I just went through?

Spirit: Yes, do you?

Chisa: Of course I do. I just did it.

Spirit: Do you really?

Chisa: When do I get to rest?

Spirit: After you have looked.

Chisa: After I look? Look where? Look back? What for? Look back over my life? Don't want to. I know what I did.

Worn down by the gentle persistent voice and the awesome presence of Spirit, Chisa begins to yield. She really had worked herself into a tizzy. She was so far from her power these last days that it was the right thing to do, to pass over.

Chisa explained in a heavy outpouring: There are White people all over the plains and hills. They bring many new diseases and dark habits. They don't know a thing about the sacred prophecies. They're entirely inferior and yet they're strong. They're taking lives. They're destroying the land. Starvation of the Spirit has taken hold in the people of the Great Turtle Island. They are threatening—a deadly force.

Spirit: Was this not prophesied?

Chisa sighs and agrees: Yes, Spirit, but I don't like to see the polarizing of good and bad into separate groups. The negativity there is swelling like a great storm on the sea. One day the Earth will not be able to balance these forces, and all will be overtaken by the Earth's own violent reply. The energy is stretching like a taut bow ready to fly its arrow. Yes, this has been prophesied, but this saddens me to see the proliferation of darkness and the Light fading. I thought I would be able to change the darkness. I am sick with it.

Spirit: Chisa, are you afraid, afraid of the future there?

With tears forming upon her eyes like dew glistening across the landscape in the rising sun, Chisa admits she is afraid for what she sees coming: the lack of soft loving hearts, gentleness, and reverence among the people.

Spirit: Let's visit the tribe.

Chisa hesitates, then looks, and describes what she sees: They are all my children. Yep, that's them. That's why I'm tired. I gave them everything I had to give. My job is done and I'm gone.

Spirit: Look into their hearts. What do you see?

Chisa slowly comprehends why Great Sprit wants her to look back: They're full. Look at that! I see love and compassion and wisdom in the hearts of the tribe. In every one. Every single one has love and compassion and wisdom. They are beautiful people. They all learned. They all have it. Even the ones I gave up on! A soft, pink energy connects their hearts and reaches all the way to you, Great Spirit.

My friend the great medicine healer, Talking Bird—where *is* my Talking Bird? Why, she's in our canyon calling to me. She wonders how I am. I'm sending her a bird that will fly close enough to startle her. No sense in leaving her with any doubt that I hear her.

Spirit: I see your humor is returning.

Chisa: Thank you, Spirit, you know I can't stay away from the civilizations for long, but sometimes I just get sick and tired and struggle. Oh, look, Talking Bird is standing on my power rock at the waterfall. She feels alone and somewhat sad. Lighten up, Medicine Woman! The bat I sent is swooping down at her and she almost loses her balance. She sees the bat, all right, and she knows I am with her. I'll just jiggle that rock a little for extra emphasis. *Ah Ha Ha Ha!* Oh, quit sputtering, the cool water feels good this time of year. *Ah Ha Ha Ha!*

Spirit: Chisa, what about the others? What does that tell you?

Chisa: They learned well.

Spirit: What else?

Chisa admits: I did well, too. It was hard work. It was a heavy responsibility. I guess I could say we succeeded. We showed the way to love and Light and knowledge to each one. It was easy with your help, but I forgot that you were here to make me succeed. When things got too dark and difficult, for too long, I got lost from you. I gave up. You were here for me. It was supposed to stay easy.

I see I carried life like a burden. It could have been my joy. I lost my lightheartedness. I now am free of the heaviness of Earth and can feel the joy again. I am overcome. Deeply touched. Thank you, Great Spirit. It was a very great responsibility I had. My tribe walks brightly on the Earth. They are a bright spot even from here. Some will walk with us here, soon. Others have long lines of energy in front of them—futures yet to be.

How much fun I lost when I lost the joy! I cheated myself. I am reminded to keep a light heart. Just the same, next time, I think I'll raise *one* child, instead of a tribe. And next time, I want to carry the Light like a baton in my hand. I want to run across all the lands carrying the Light and joy of Spirit.

Spirit: And so you will. Now rest here with me, my child. Be replenished. Be of good spirit for you are my child and I love you.

✳

The Healing

Reunion with Great Spirit is a joy like no other. It is a return to the source of love and perfection. I understand that it calmed Chisa, brought back her humor, and gave her a fresh perspective on life. Wouldn't it be nice to embody these benefits while we're living?

I still tend to wear myself down and get 'sick and tired and struggle,' just like Chisa. Her message of keeping a light step is more valuable than I realized when I first visited her lifetime. Becoming aware that I can heavy-up any given moment, I realize now that I can also consciously lighten-up any moment. It is all about choices, attitude, and keeping a strong connection to Great Spirit.

A big part of lightening up is spending time with my special friends, such as Professor Sandra (Sandy) Ridgely in this lifetime, also known as Talking Bird!

I remember the day I met her and the decades of goofy fun we have had since then such as adults rarely permit themselves. We laugh, we cry, we travel and shop; and we meditate, make shields, and grow along our spiritual paths with the company of each other. I can see now that our friendship is an echo of the friendship I witnessed in my Native American past lifetime as Chisa.

In the early 1990s fax machines and computers entered our lives to help us keep pace with the speeding up of time. FedEx® and other overnight delivery services were already zooming around the globe. For me, it was time to learn desktop publishing, so I enrolled in a college course that met on Saturday mornings throughout the spring semester and required hours of work each week in the computer lab.

I was nervous the first day of class—because I was always nervous with new things—but was awestruck by the presence of the professor. I labeled her Earth Mama. Well into the semester, I arrived at class early to work on the computer. I was drafting a flyer advertising my first Shield Workshop that I would hold a month later attended by 10 people. I manipulated the graphics and had three feathers, stars, triangles, and a circle of the shield design that would later become my logo.

Professor Ridgely moved around the room answering questions and chatting with students before class started. (This was back in the day when everyone had to learn the difference between 'left click' and 'right click.') She stopped next to me and seemingly yelled in her booming teacher voice, "What is that?" *Oh, jeez.* I explained it was a flyer for a meditation workshop I was planning. She replied, "I'm interested in that. I would like to do it."

I was shocked! Of all the courses offered, how could I sign up for *this* course at *this* time with *this* professor? I must have had behind-the-scenes help from the Guides! That is how things happen in my life.

The Adventures of Sandy and Louise

So began the adventures of Sandy and Louise. Sandy has made more shields than anyone else with me—we both have done a lot of healing work! Two other key points about Sandy are: she likes to shop and is footloose—she likes to travel—and therein lies the opportunity for our adventures. As part of our shared desire to escape suburban life and pursue our spiritual journeys, we took numerous trips to Arizona, New Mexico, and Colorado.

She was with me on the trip where I was bitten by the brown recluse spider and spent the week in a venom- and drug-induced stupor—my initiation as a Spider Woman.

On another trip, we returned to our cabin one afternoon to find a raccoon clinging to some lattice by the deck. He looked at us and we looked at him. We stopped to ponder what he was doing there in broad daylight, our hands loaded with packs and supplies from our outing. In a split second, a lurking mountain lion screamed and leapt at the raccoon, sending the raccoon flying onto the roof and into hiding somewhere. The lion disappeared, unsuccessful in her chase, but she stalked the area for the duration of our stay. Her musky scent wafted in through the screened windows each night. We were blissfully nonchalant on these trips and simply ignored the threat on the other side of the flimsy screen.

This reminds me of how aware I was on our trips that I was different away from my role as wife, mother, marketing consultant, and local newspaper columnist for the environment—slipping the bonds of responsibilities.

During our travels Sandy was outgoing, meeting everyone on the plane sitting near our seats, knowing our waiters and waitresses very well before the meals were over, and she was every shopkeepers' new best friend. I, on the other hand, was inward and quiet. I kept notes of messages and insights; she collected friends, art, and souvenirs. Both of us ate, slept, hiked, and took photographs.

True to form, on a trip to the Navajo and Hopi reservations in Arizona, as we left breakfast one morning she said, "The waitress told me where the Dineh (Navajo People) go. When we drive toward the Hopi reservation today, we will see a windmill on the left and an old rodeo grounds next to a dirt road. We should take the dirt road."

"To where?" I asked. "To the place where the Dineh go." Like I said, nonchalance wins over logic on these trips, so it sounded good to me. Not long after, we saw the windmill and turned on the dirt road. Our rental car bounced on its shock absorbers up and down through potholes and dips, kicking up a cloud of dust visible for miles around on the flat, desert horizon. We were wild and free. Laughing at our adventure, I thought, *Jim would not take his family on the unfamiliar, unpaved, 'road.' He would worry about a flat tire, or worse.* Sandy and I laughed, our sunglasses bounced on our faces, and suddenly we were at the end of the road! *Yikes!* I slammed on the brakes, diverting a possible Thelma-and-Louise moment. Just in front of the car was a canyon rim. It was breathtaking. Desert sand and sagebrush gave way to rock and space. Sandstone strata of blue, white, and orange-red revealed through eons of erosion and exposure.

We stayed for an hour, clearing our energy fields, thinking we ought to be as pure as possible to visit the Hopi reservation. Being fair-skinned tourists in the hot desert sun, we slathered on suntan lotion and pulled on straw hats before getting comfortable on the ground for a good long look. Truthfully, Sandy had brought a collection of hats and she chose a straw one, too.

Above the wide, curving horizon was a sky of blues and turquoise that seemed to permit the cirrus clouds and thunderheads to pass through. We watched storm clouds gather in the distance and drop rain. Rain bans formed in the sun's rays. Ravens drifted in on the thermals, keeping an opportunistic eye on the canyon. Some of the photos show possible UFO-looking things up in the clouds—maybe someone was watching us watch the canyon!

Back in the car and feeling refreshed, we continued eastward to the Hopi reservation, a seemingly poor, dismal, disappointing, maybe even scary place. But we were not fooled by such shabby appearances. The Hopi hold the secrets of existence.

Sandy arranged a "tour" with the one Native who offered service. There was no discussion of the sacred part of their life, only references to historical traditions. We understood the protective façade presented to us as outsiders.

As we stood near a cliff near the site of a kiva, Sandy listened intently and asked questions of the tour guide, serving as a good distraction, while my attention turned to the view behind us. A wide canyon lay open with walls dropping away for hundreds of feet. I had a vision. *Ah, ha!* I saw them—the Kachina Spirits. They were huge, towering over the canyon, appearing as hazy formations, dancing and making themselves visible to these eyes. What a thrill! Kachina representations sold in shops are usually small, belying the truth of the Kachina Spirits and the magnitude of their power. I watched and laughed until the tour was over.

We crossed the dusty reservation to use an outhouse that had no door (*Why not? We are on an adventure trip and we cannot do this everywhere!*), and departed. We stopped at the blue canyon to cleanse our energy again. Then back to the motel to get dinner and, I am sure, more guidance from our waiter.

Before I proceed with the next story, I must mention several more points about Sandy I came to know: she is a fast driver and has a Guide that gets her front row parking spaces. These are both good traits in a traveling partner, especially when airports and timetables are involved.

Another trait presented itself during a trip to Sedona, Arizona. Possibly *the* most conflicted moment of our travels—that I can always hold over her head—occurred when we walked to the top of one of the vortexes as the sun was dropping in the sky. We were really on top of a small mound—in my opinion—but it was at this moment that she decided to tell me she was afraid of heights. I did not see the relevance of this, because we were not up high, in my mind, and it was out of character with her suggestion to go hiking out West in the first place.

She became somewhat hysterical, afraid she was going to fall off a cliff. I thought s*he has to be joking! What cliff?* She cried and stressed all the way down to the parking lot. Dust kicked up on our shoes as we slid/walked down the mound as night fell. She was angry. I still did not understand what was going on with her. She told me she was serious. Then I realized. It was that death-over-the-canyon-cliff past life that arose in her. It is a meditation that she thinks about and fears. I had one of those falling down-the-canyon deaths, too. It *is* a painful way to go, as death is not instantaneous. Her memory had an emotional hold on her still. And it continued to have a hold on her at the Grand Canyon, where I ended up hiking alone down below the rim. The description of the trail *below the rim* was all it took for us to know I would hike alone. She shopped instead. It is not easy to find flat, cliff-less trails in the West, but we have succeeded in finding a few! Sandy, Sandy, Sandy!

Now you are ready to hear the best Sandy and Louise story. We flew from scorching, sticky hot Baltimore/Washington International Airport one August day into high and dry Denver International Airport, secured the four-wheel-drive rental, and headed out for experiences unknown. My head pounded from dehydration as I acclimated. Sandy was blissful. She had already met numerous new people. The trip took us to Boulder, up the Front Range through Rocky Mountain National Park and eventually, to the Park exit at Grand Lake. This is where we spent the final days of the visit, in the scenic and wondrous Montane and Subalpine life zones.

This day, we prepared to be gone at least an entire morning on a hike up to Black Rain's mountain meadow, packing water and snacks for sustenance and pen and paper for note taking. This was the culmination of our trip—seeking shield visions. We climbed up through the woods and along the swift-flowing creek. Further ahead, the trail exited the woods and bordered the meadow which was divided by the meandering, fish-filled stream. Arriving with anticipation and excitement, we were not disappointed.

Connecting with Nature around us, we focused our meditative eyes on the surrounding scenery. Bald mountaintops, tree lines on soaring peaks, lodgepole pine forests, grasses and wildflowers, moose, chipmunks, and butterflies. A clear, deep blue sky, which is the Colorado calling card.

We set up a resting place in the shade and got comfortable on the ground. The occasional backpacker or group of hikers passed, sharing remarks with Sandy about the beauty of the place. I nodded or smiled, but remained contemplative and prayerful. We waited expectantly. And waited some more.

Then, the most surprising thing happened. It was startling and hilarious. Our message did not come from the plants and animals around us. It came, literally, from above! We looked up to the sky and words and pictures were forming in white cumulus clouds. We were dumbfounded! We laughed and laughed. What a treat this was!

Familiar and unfamiliar faces appeared in the clouds. They formed messages and shapes for Sandy's shield design. Spirit, speaking to her in her computerese language, wrote with the clouds: *www.whisperingwind.* How could this be? It is magical. Sandy's name is related to the element air and it is written in the sky! How perfect! Sandy received her Native American name, Whispering Wind, and her shield vision. We stayed for hours, not wanting to miss a moment of excitement and wanting this jubilee to last forever. We kept wondering, *how is it that no one else can see these formations in the sky?*

A young backpacker came bouncing down the trail. He was jaunty with nice energy. He stopped to talk with Sandy. After he went on his way, she said, "Did you see that? Did you read his Tee-shirt?" I replied that I had not. She revealed, "It said: when all is said and done, all there is, is One."

"Ah! That's the message of *my* shield!" I screamed. And we laughed some more. I wrote it down, wondering if he was real, or an apparition! The Guides were having such fun with us that day! We agreed no one would believe us, if we described what had happened, which made it even more special.

Black Rain and the tribe emerged from the forest. Walking with him were both his daughters of long ago, Sandy and Louise. We have been sisters for a long time. He remained visible only long enough to acknowledge our presence, then retreated back into the void. The magic and shield seeking were over. We packed up and walked back down the trail.

That evening, as I worked on my shield in our cabin near a creek, Black Rain reappeared on the boulders outside. I was aware of his presence and went out to observe him striking a warrior's pose, professing his love and support for me, with arm raised toward the heavens. Indescribable, sacred love. My heart caught and filled with his devotion. His heart beat against mine, pushing away the clouds of doubt that clutter my experience. Yes, I *feel* the love. I *can* feel it.

My father, on the other side in Spirit, joined him in this uncharacteristic display of love. A great healing happened for me. To experience the flow of love from my father for the first time revealed that he had healed himself and was able to share his heart with me, finally, and that I had healed enough to receive and feel his love, too. This event is so significant, that I pause as I write this to take the beauty of its truth deeper within me. Imagine, the one strongest soul you have lived with and fought with over the ages, the one that brought the most challenges to you—for the sake of your strengthening and growth—and that the two of you find peace and love for one another ... at a mountain stream with water lapping noisily over the rocks ... All there is, is One.

Sandy and I left the next day, headed down to the airport, and flew back to sea level. We made a memory and had a great time, as friends should do.

The zaniness of friendship gets me through this challenging life on Earth. Friendships with familiar souls, who remind me of Home, can carry from one lifetime to the next. *This* love never dies, either. Whispering Wind and Laughing Waters will be together again—not only for next year's adventure—but also as we travel the web of time, of this I am sure. *Ho!* In the meantime, I will rely on these memories and experiences to lighten up!

Yes, laughter is a part of living well!

... And in this lifetime, as requested of Spirit, I have one child and carry the scepter of a Chaticks-si-Chaticks warrior—the baton of Light that in my hand becomes the pen to ink these stories of transforming life across this land! Thank you, Still Waters! Thank you, Great Spirit, for answering my prayers.

George's Interlude

Yes, laughter is their natural state. Sometimes they need reminding of this. We Guides are happy to oblige!

Louise, her husband, and her son have lived and worked together on soul lessons over many lifetimes. There have been mistakes and she has another chance to get it right this lifetime. The dance of anger threatens the makings of a joyous lifetime. All the moments of anger are lost moments of love and compassion. Will they support each other enough to get rid of the anger, fear, and self-blame for past mistakes? Let us take a look.

ഉ൙ന

11

Peace Begins With Me

I YEARNED TO BE IN THE Rocky Mountains. In the higher place where new adventures called to me. Pulled there like a magnet, I collaborated with Jim to plan our first Colorado family vacation. We did some research, but mostly followed our instincts in making reservations, meaning we were Guided. This was my first visit to the lake and meadow that Sandy and I revisited later. As soon as the Mitchell's—Jim, Matt, and I—arrived at the destination lake, I knew a piece of my past lay in the water. I could not remember how I got there, but the connection was undeniable.

Unable to sleep the first night of the visit, I wrapped myself in a blanket and went outside to sit by the lake. The midnight moon appeared and disappeared behind quickly moving clouds. Mesmerized, I received a vivid and clear shield vision from my Guides.

I sensed they were with me, as if a gathering was happening. I opened myself to the sacred moment, but the glare and reflection of inn lights interfered with my concentration and clarity. I thought *it would be nice if the lights were not on*, and almost instantly, the lights went out. Not all of them, just the ones in front of me that were the most bothersome. Startled by this response from the Universe, I continued to connect with the surface of the water, the forested Rocky Mountains rising up out of the water, the wide, star-filled sky above, and the dance of swiftly moving clouds.

This place had been your home, I heard. *Indian times. Family. A joyous life. Then tragedy. The canoe. The weather.* I resisted the truth and could not go deeply into the memory. While the memory remained vague, the connection to the place was strong.

Suddenly, like a huge cloud filling the sky, Spirit reached down to me with long arms open and presented three symbols across the wide wingspan of Eagle: a peace pipe with a wolf on it, an eagle in flight, and a bear with a heart line. Then all together, they faded into the dark summer sky, leaving only the stars and moon. The vivid vision left me awestruck! Stunned! The lights clicked on and snapped me back to the here and now. This is what I love, love, love about my spiritual path: personal encounters with Spirit and the challenge to assimilate the experiences!

The next morning Jim, Matt, and I hiked up a short trail through the lodge pole pines along a flowing creek that fed the lake. My East Shield meditation of the night before was on my mind. I fell in love with the place protected by the upright lodge poles. The water was clear and sparkled and rushed noisily over the boulders dropping to the lake below. I continued to feel strongly connected to this place and could have chosen to stay forever. As we walked a little further, the trail suddenly left the woods and opened up to a high mountain meadow surrounded by tall gray peaks that touched the turquoise sky. *Magical!*

Fish glistened in the stream; short, medium, and tall wildflowers flecked the scene with color; and my breathing caught. My heart nearly stopped as I stood frozen in the beauty of this peaceful, open space that exists beyond the woods. *Such delight!* The stream was still, surrounded by tall grasses. It was from this calm place of still water that the lake waters originated. I soaked up as much of the energy there as I could. If there is heaven on Earth, this is it.

This is your Spirit Home, I heard a voice say, *where peace and beauty live beyond the fear and anger.* Black Rain and his tribe emerged from the line of pine trees across the meadow. They greeted us and let me know they still hold the energy needed for humankind in the heart of this mountain meadow. And I saw walking behind him, his daughter—daughter of the chief—and it was me. *This is where Black Rain lives! This is where I first saw you in meditation with arm raised, beseeching me to seek higher. I have found you. I am Home!* I have returned to the meadow many times since then.

Later, down at the lake, Matt was most enthusiastic about renting a boat and Jim was up for it. I, on the other hand, was not interested in renting a motor boat and going out on that deep water. It was challenging enough for me just to sit by the lake, let alone go out on it! But, two votes to one. *What's wrong with the shore,* I wonder, as the rental is made and we step into the boat.

We did not encounter any trouble; I did not die; but I did not have fun. Jim and Matt, on the other hand, were the picture of happiness and the photos show it. The wind is blowing against them; their hair is flying; water is splashing in the air; the sky is filled with huge white clouds; and light is shining on their shoulders. In one photo, Black Rain appears in a cloud over the lake with his arm raised in joyous celebration. *What is he so happy about?* I wonder.

✱

The history that Spirit tried to show me that first night by the lake came through later when I was ready to know. In my meditation I am high in the Rocky Mountains on the shores of the glacial lake. Smoke curls rise from teepees into the crisp gray air as the snow-laden sky drops lower into the peaks surrounding the Indian village. With the unexpected temperature falling, skies darkening, and winds rising across the surface of the lake, members of the tribe know that an unseasonal storm is approaching and tend to preparations for its arrival. A dare spreads quietly through the group of bold, foolhardy, young scouts, who launch their wood canoes and paddle out onto the lake to test their skills in the white-capped, rough waters. A thin cover of snow is already on the ground. More snow is coming.

The wind is making it harder to see with clarity, creating tension and confusion. I cannot find my son. He is one of the young braves out on the water. My search changes from concern to frantic. *Where is he?* I cannot locate his canoe or the other scouts and canoes. Will they withstand the current, the wind, and the cold? Their excitable fighting spirit undoubtedly creates a dangerous game.

Among the trees on the shore, everyone is busy as the storm drops into the village obscuring visibility. One person is upset. It is me. My husband did not *let* our son go in the canoe, but I blame him anyway. I rant and rave next to our lodge. The fringes and furs of my garments flap as my arms flail in the air dramatically. My face is red with the heat of anger and the sting of icy wind. Fear pounds through me—not all the canoes have returned. Some are feared lost. My husband does not respond to my yelling. He stands weak and silent like a beaten man. He blames himself even though I am foolish to tell him that it is his fault.

I storm away and get in a canoe myself—rash and impatient. My fear and rage at the possible loss of our son blind my sensibilities.

The storm is powerful. The hard winds blow in gusts. There is no visibility. Everything is white with pelting snow. I call out for him and keep paddling. I hear no answer—I would recognize his voice—that resonance I love. I would know it anywhere. I see no one and cannot even guess which way would be back to the camp's shore.

The fear and exertion start to take a toll on my strength. My heated rage subsides, worn down by the cold blowing through my garments. My skin is becoming raw, and my calls to him are weakening.

Weeping and lost, I am too numb to keep hold of the paddle. It slips away into the whiteout and I cry. *The elders said I was so hot headed and foolish and that would get me in trouble. I am lost in the storm. My love is back on the shore. How can I get back to him? My child, where is he? I want us to be together.*

Hoping to protect myself from the elements, I lie down in the canoe and hide my face from the frigid wind. With no guidance, the canoe lurches and pitches. *How does it happen that one freezes to death? What is the last sensation—physical pain, numbness? No, it is despair.*

I am barely conscious when the canoe tips and rolls me into the water. There my frozen body sinks to be claimed by the lake.

My Spirit rises from the waters and moves to the shore. Our son, who had returned safely, stands in sorrow and guilt and anguish with his father, who never forgives himself for the tragedy that befell his family that day. The snow continues drifting. The cold freezes the hearts of the young brave and his father. For the rest of his lifetime, I could hear his heartbreaking cries as wild as the night cries of the lone wolf, echoing from canyon walls.

I weep for the pain I caused and vow to make up it up to them. Next time I will be more peaceful, trusting, and loving.

✱

The Healing

My emotional/behavioral healing has come a long way. I do not have as many layers of turbulence anymore, and I continue to work on calming the inner waters. My spirit must also heal. To help with this evolution, I use shield making. Taking the emotional tenor, colors, actions, and images from the lakeside vision, I make my East Shield representing the path to illumination.

On a dark blue background representing the midnight sky, I lay sparkles for the stars and a round, opalescent shell for the moon. With a fine net fabric I cut out the shape of spirit reaching down to me with open arms to give me my gifts. These gifts are clues to my future path to enlightenment. I place the three symbols across the shield. First, is a peace pipe with a wolf on it. The peace pipe, meaning inner peace, and the wolf, symbolizing a teacher. Then the eagle in flight, a soaring symbol of Great Spirit. Finally, the bear with a heart line, representing my goals for healing and all who can hear my message.

I am not proud of the rage and mistakes I have brought to relationships. The process of making the shield and meditating with it, reminds me of the power, support, and guidance available for healing on the spiritual level. Divine inspiration for living a better life is available when I open to it.

Six more years have passed since our family vacation to the lake with our young son. Dinosaurs and boats do not clutter the bath tub at home anymore. Our son has grown and developed an interest in nature; to wit, a flea experiment sits on the dining room table providing the answer to the question, *Can fleas and ants live together in a Ziploc® bag?* The pet gerbils and snake have been laid to rest in the back yard next to the hedge. His snails keep reproducing, as do his slugs (kept outside). The family cocker spaniel gets most of his hugs now, instead of Mom. He is 11 and declares his interest in white water kayaking.

> GEORGE: She has not developed trust around the water, yet, and his interest will push her to improve this.

Very cleverly, my response to his request is to research the sport first. Read about it before actually doing it. We learn that traditionally a Native American boy was taken out in a kayak on his 12th birthday to celebrate his passage to manhood and to learn to fish and paddle. Strengthening his case, the books all agree that kayaking is much easier than canoeing and is a sport for everyone! *Oh, great! This plan backfired!*

So, on his 12th birthday, I stand at the edge of the Potomac River on the Maryland side, inspecting the high water at near flood stage. I am terrified of the water's force. We learn that the Potomac is the home of most members of the U.S. kayaking team, because this river rises and falls and changes so rapidly that it provides endless challenges to test their skill. *Great!* All my fears rise. The force of the river is indomitable, unpredictable.

From where does he get the desire to go out on the water? How can he be so carefree? I postpone the lesson for one week to give the river time to subside, which it does. And then I let him go, because the desire beats in his heart. It is where he is powerful and free and happy.

He is about one-third the age and size of everyone else in the class. He fastens the waterproof skirt to the kayak, takes his paddle in his hand, and slides his vessel into the current. He hits his stroke and spins in circles, right then left. He glides across the surface. He feels the power of the river beneath him as a friendly force. He has no hesitation. He simply enjoys himself, and yells, "You have to try this, Mom!" *Yeah, right. You will never find me in a kayak on a roaring river or in a canoe on a big lake.* Yet, I am aware of the warmth washing over me that comes from his joy.

Over time he learns the basic rolls, runs some chutes, and generally enjoys himself. On another occasion, he is out with his instructor. They paddle up the river and out of sight in early evening. The sun is setting now and casting a golden glow against the rock cliffs on either side of the river. The surrounding darkness increases. I struggle to stay focused on the beautiful scene around me. The groups are returning to the shore. *Where is his group?* Each helmeted kayaker and each kayak seem to resemble him, but each turns out to be someone else.

Please, God, return him to me, safe and whole and unharmed.
Please, God, return him to me, safe and whole and unharmed.
Please, God, return him to me, safe and whole and unharmed.

I pray out of fear and anxiety for his protection and for his safe return. I work determinedly to replace panic with self-control and display no outward ranting or rage.

It is nearly full sundown and hard to see, but he appears in front of my eyes! He *does* return! Tired and happy, having met the challenge and enjoyed the adventure. I greet him calmly, able to pretend I had not worried at all.

> GEORGE: She chose prayer over outright panic. Matt taught her this, finally! He will re-test her every so often, for it is his job to work with the lesson of remaining peaceful, especially when it is difficult, not just when it is easy. Reader, what does your child teach you? What fear and drama do you bring into relationships in place of peace and trust?

Yes, if you are wondering, I did go in a canoe one day! Just days after the 2005 Hurricane Katrina made landfall in Florida, across the Gulf Coast, and through Louisiana, causing death and destruction of epic proportions, Jim paddled our rented canoe up the stagnant, tranquil waters of the C&O Canal near the Potomac River. Water was on my mind and heart. This was the right time to get back into a canoe.

As I took my seat in the canoe, I went into a state of fear and barely breathed. Somehow, the canoe turned around and I sat facing forward at the front, staring at the water that split and rippled around the pointed prow. I could not even see Jim without turning around, a movement that made the canoe tip a little. *Oh, God!* All I had to do was sit still, hold on, and enjoy it; but that was asking too much. The canoe rocked and pitched with every stroke of the paddle. (I figured George was shaking things up a little—testing that trust and faith!) Water slapped around our unstable metal vessel. Jim was laughing at me on the inside, and telling me to just sit still and hold on. I was tense and scared the entire ride. We made it back to the dock and I watched as I stepped both feet back onto solid ground. On my behalf, I can say I have been in a canoe—and did not even get wet!

Our son? Matt is still happiest on the water—white water rafting, kayaking, motor boating and waterskiing, jet skiing, canoeing, and swimming—and when the water is frozen—skiing and snowboarding. He continually demonstrates for me to trust that joy is in the body.

I must note that my lesson of *peace begins with me* is not mastered in a single moment or canoe ride, but when tested in life repeatedly, moment-by-moment, it is the path to returning Home to a peaceful heart where joy resides.

George's Interlude

Have you thought of the irony yet, that her Native name is
Laughing Waters? Therein, is the beauty of her challenging spiritual
journey.

We visited with the animals in an earlier story. Let's look at the
mystery of plants. Sip some relaxing tea, as you enjoy this next story
of pure existence.

80 03

12

What You Bring In,
Is All You Really Have

I REACH BACK ACROSS TIME ... before civilization created legacies and religions ... and living was primitive—less sophisticated, philosophical, and intellectual ...

Before God revealed his word to the Prophet and Messenger Muhammad ibn 'Abdullah (c. 570 - 632 AD) of Mecca,

Before Jesus of Nazareth (c. 0-33 AD) was venerated as Christ, the Son of God, and icon of Christianity,

Before the Hindus defined God as the Light of the World,

Before God revealed Judaic laws and commandments to Moses on Mount Sinai,

Before the philosopher, Confucius (c. 551-479 BC) of China professed the Golden Rule and taught men to find the path through individual study,

Before Prince Siddhartha Gautama (c. 563-483 BC) of Nepal became the Awakened or Enlightened One, teaching Buddhism as the Middle Way to Enlightenment,

Before the philosopher, Lao-Tzu (c. 604-531 BC) of China pointed the way to Taoism and identified the yin and yang, five elements, five flavors, five colors, and five modes.

My memory takes me back on the Earth before all these times—long before these revered men offered their pathways to generations of humankind—back to the Age of Stone.

I did not hunt animals or eat their meat. When the tribe moved across the lands to find new, rich hunting grounds or better conditions, I moved with them, but my attention remained on the landscape. I was a gatherer. Would there be familiar plants that I would know from before? Would there be new plants whose secrets had not yet been revealed? I was curious about their color, height, length, strength, softness, succulence, scent, texture, hairiness, and where they thrived and which ones appeared near each other. I had learned that some plants would grow near each other, favoring the same place. If I found one, would I find the other? Jittery excitement about what I might discover fueled my steps on these tribal moves, just as the hope for shelter and animal herds fueled my fellow clan members.

My days were consumed with plants. Finding, gathering, and preparing plants. The memory fills me now with joy and touches my passion. I was harmonious with the land, had vision and could see fire and Light, carried ecstasy and felt Spirit creating inside me. The core of my being was fully exposed. Life was simple with a lack of pretenses.

✱

I move each day through the land of the tribe guided internally by Spirit from one plant to another. Spirit's voice speaks to me in sounds and in pictures. He tells me about the plants. I learn how to select plants or plant parts for picking, when and how to harvest them, how to prepare them, and how the tribe can use them. The various plants are food, spices, and medicines. This is so natural for me that I wonder why everyone else does not know this. But they do not. Tribe members watch me, confer about me, and worry about me. They never interfere and never stop me. I can see their concern for my welfare, but I do not feel their fear or anxiety. I am protected from their negativity. They do not understand, but they let me be. This life is adventurous, experimental, and joyous. The song of my life is composed of inner inspiration and guidance, rather than from the customs around me.

Standing in silence by a plant, I experience a magnetic connection with it and hear the voice of wisdom. I am content and welcome the feeling of freedom that comes when I focus on the plants and listen for the voice. My work is play.

This plant is ZsuZsu, the voice says. *It is the vine that connects all.* The clue to the value of this plant, Spirit teaches, is its heart-shaped leaves. Its leaves are bright red, polished, and leathery alternating along the thin, square vine. It will be gone one day, but many souls will recall it. From the male plants, I learn to make a tea that enlivens the spirit. It wakes up, energizes, and strengthens the user. It gives leaders the inner strength to lead, mothers the endless strength to nurture, and hunters enduring strength to track and kill and carry their prey. *ZsuZsu* is for the heart of the people. It makes you full of yourself, so you are peaceful with others. You are satisfied, balanced, energized, and calm.

Its brown infusion is sipped. I briefly boil the plant stems and pray over the steaming liquid, asking the plant energy to connect with the best part of the person ingesting it. The plant grows abundantly across the ground in sunny areas in low places, so I am able to find it easily; yet, the sight of the plant means nothing to others compared to the sight of a mammoth or even a smaller animal. *ZsuZsu* provides what no animal meat can provide—the energy of life.

The *Ulu* plant has a thick white stalk underground that heals the skin of tribal members. It heals burns, sores, abrasions, and rashes, working from within when sipped as a tea decoction and externally when applied in a fibrous wrap. The *Ulu* plant has large green, prickly leaves with thick meaty stalks. I learn to carefully hold onto the plant and uproot it without scratching myself. Spirit explains that the pain this plant can cause, is the very thing it heals. I gently tap, not pound, the cut stalks on a rock with a rounded stone in my hand to bring the juices from within up to the surface. This flattened, fibrous piece is placed over the injured skin. It is soothing and cool even on open wounds. Some of the mashed stalks are chewed to ingest the juices. *Ulu* is important to the health of clan members. It grows in wet, lush areas only, so I carry a supply of it when we move to higher ground.

The lovely, tall green bush with arrow-shaped leaves and sweetly scented purple spike flowers induces romantic feelings when smelled. Spirit warns that although this plant is pleasurable to see and smell, it is deadly to ingest. *Simply enjoy it as it grows*, he warns, *for the pleasure it brings.*

Another plant with lavender flowers grows much shorter and in drier places. It has an earthy sweet smell that affects the women and men differently. In women, it enhances romantic feelings and helps them desire the physical penetration of their mates. For men, it cools the angry fire that burns inside them. It relaxes their temperament and calms tensions that grow among the aggressive men. I dry the plant leaves and square stems and burn them, so the smoke wafts around the fire pit and cave area when clan members rest, talk, and work. Again, the scent when inhaled promotes peaceful relations and healing.

The fire pit is the central gathering place for tribal members. As is customary, they sit nearby in groups to eat the hot meals of animal meat. I sit in my group that includes my mother and as usual I do not eat my serving. The clan tolerates my oddities, but treats me suspiciously. They motion about me right in front of me, as if I cannot see. They wonder, *how can she survive without eating more? What should we do with her portion of food. Who should eat it?* They know no other way to live than by the clan rules and customs. Even when they witness it in front of their own eyes, day in and day out, they cannot understand what keeps me alive.

There is a world of unlimited plant life (flowers, fruits, berries, seeds, leaves, stems, bark, and roots) and unlimited uses and benefits for the tribe. How absolutely thrilling and joy-making this is for me. I love these plants. I love hearing the voice and learning about these plants. I love living this way every day.

Some clan members wake each day to the warmth of the fire, some to the sight of fresh hides and carcasses, but no other wakes to the contentment and pleasure that come with the first sight of plants in the landscape.

One day, I see beyond the herbs hanging to dry at the cave opening out over the miles of vegetation. With my back to the dark side of the cave and my face toward the opening, I look upon a male form that appears, nearly filling the cave opening and silhouetted in shadow by the bright light resting on his left shoulder. So blinding is the light behind him that I cannot see his features. *What name is his? Who is this?* The energy emanating from this God is indescribable. We communicate fully without speaking, as if he is inside my heart and head. I know he is not a clan member, but the Spirit of the voice and wisdom I so often hear. He steps back to leave, and I pull on him with my energy to stay. The wind blows gently. He will go. *Don't leave me, don't ever leave me.* He visits me in the night like a mate and more, filling my heart and senses, then leaves. His memory lingers in the lavender bundle that sways in the breeze of his departure.

✱

GEORGE: To know the experience of the shadow/mate, is to have union with the Universe and embrace it in your heart.

Louise has known. She has always known from the beginning how to unlock secrets of life. She only has to remember the bundle of purple-flowered plants hanging in the cave, swinging in the breeze, to feel her internal spiritual union.

Her name was Uma. She was unique in her tribe. Her bed is a large brown fur animal skin. Her hot weather clothing is a deer-like skin—lightweight and loose. A medicine bundle of soft animal skin and fur hangs around her neck, over her heart. Near her, plants lie and hang in bunches and bundles, tied with sinew, stringy bark, or animal hair. Each plant is useful and important.

The knowledge of how to use the herbs is both natural instinct and learned talent. The future survival of her tribe depends on her ability to gather and cure the herbs and on her astute use of each known remedy. She has the wisdom of an aged one, yet feels very young—childlike and playful. She dares to be different, living on plants, but there is no *daring* to it for her, as she simply is true to herself. Uma is not different through anger or defiance. She lives her personal essence, knows no other way to be, and lives an inner life in the outside world.

Uma is a great value to the tribe. What she knows, does, and shares contributes to her their health and well-being. She lives a higher life among the people, seeding new traditions joyously, freely, quietly, and is not dependent emotionally on any relationships within the tribe. Uma cultivates, naturally and easily, the inner connection to Spirit and is in union with the voice of guidance—the voice that vibrates through the nature of plant life.

In the springtime of 1994, I attended my first modern herb festival at a large, wooded urban park in Baltimore. All along a half-mile loop through the park were stationed different herb vendors selling their products—everything from herb plants to herbal cures to books and knick-knacks. I spent some time with my own healer at her booth and some time wandering around. Everyone there—all ages, all kinds—was connected through their interest in herbs. It was a peaceful, quiet festival.

As I departed and drove my car off the grassy parking area and onto the paved street, I was overtaken by the most captivating charged energy. *My lavender man!* He pulled me from my body for ecstatic play in the Universe. The joyous uplifting from my roots released into the sparkling universal consciousness. We rode together through wildness and freedom to Oneness.

I then found myself back in my physical body once again, driving down a now unfamiliar city street, and laughed aloud in the afterglow wondering, *who is that lavender man? Who is my friend from herbal times? He is one with me, my lavender Man-Spirit.*

I remember as a young child standing next to the lilac bush in the back yard. *How long did I stand there inhaling its charm and staring at its somehow familiar appearance?* I had favorite places in the yard for tumbling and cartwheels, for badminton, swinging, and tree-climbing, but this was the place where I stood still.

And that odd plant that grew in my aunt's back yard captivated me the same way. On a hot Wisconsin morning, I stood transfixed as if seeing an old friend unexpectedly. Something seemed familiar. *What plant was this,* I wondered. *Rhubarb,* was the answer. *It did not look like something to make a pie from ... a pie ... this plant was picked for pie? That doesn't seem right.* That did not make sense and I struggled with sensing an old connection.

When I was by myself during that childhood summer vacation, I stood near the bed of rhubarb and walked around it several times. There was something magnetic about the rhubarb patch. I was distracted by the wind that swayed the white bed sheets hanging nearby on the laundry line. Rhubarb in the ground with its magenta stalks and substantial leaves, I reflected, the laundry waving, resting, then snapping in the wind, and ... rhubarb pie. Everyone else seemed to agree with the custom of planting rhubarb and making it into pie. That was food for thought!

As an adult, I created an herb and meditation garden in my own back yard. Alone for the weekend, I managed to find the strength and energy to clear the space that for years had been the vegetable garden, till the soil, enrich it with humus and peat moss, shop for stepping stones, move in a Buddha statue, and select and plant herbs. I did all this with no forethought. I was spontaneously guided. I felt I *knew* why I chose some plants—lavender, rosemary, thyme, mint, lemongrass, sage. I included several wildflowers that grew in the foothills and mountain meadows of Black Rain's tribe—Indian paintbrush, columbine, bee balm, and yarrow. But one herb in particular I thought I chose because its appearance contrasted with the others. It was rue and several years would pass before the secret of rue was known to me and the real uses it would have. During that time I was curious about it, walked around it, weeded around it, and—needing to have a purpose for its being there—decided it symbolized all that remained unknown to me.

GEORGE: We had given Louise a little reminder of the spiritual ecstasy available to her. The lavender man was the Red bloodline of the Red Light that lives closest to the Earth, seeding plant knowledge for use in times when meat is scarce.

During this lifetime, our charge has often wondered how the Native Americans knew how to use the natural world around them for food, shelter, and survival; when the information originated; and from where had it come. Now she knows how that occurs!

In this early time on Earth, Louise's connection to Spirit was strongest. She maintained the protection and connection that came with the purity of birth. She did not leave them. Joy, protection, clarity, and wisdom were her natural birthrights. Her Spirit Guide Elvie (Earth Life Giver) was Louise's primary connection, and when her work with him for the clan was done, he gently took her to where she was needed next.

Keep this in mind, Reader: What you bring into this world is all you have—and you may have it all! It is who you are. It is the energy to draw on. It is where to look for answers to your questions. You have the keys, inside. This is what Uma and Elvie teach us.

George's Interlude

Even before the time known as the Second Ice Age and the Age of Stone on the big landmasses, was the time of high civilizations of Lemuria and Atlantis. Lemuria was a peaceful place then. Atlantis was a mature and powerful place. Louise revisited both lifetimes and experienced the creative, nurturing joy of Lemuria and the suffering and catastrophic destruction of Atlantis caused by imbalances on Earth in that civilization.

ഇൻ രൂ

13

Consequences

GEORGE: Lemuria and Atlantis civilizations were beings from another universe, here to setup very sophisticated energy experiments light-years ahead of modern man. Many of those civilians are now materializing on Earth again. Some agencies are nearing the experimental points in research today that match the achievements, before the tragic loss, of Atlantis. Harnessing and using for the good of humankind the powers of crystals and stones is tantalizing to inquisitive minds and a temptation to the greedy. The lessons of Atlantis may soon be exposed from the ocean floor for rediscovery.

Before there was anything man-made on Earth, there was the stone of Earth itself. Living, breathing stone, recording vibrations of creation, power, love, peace, harmony, and enlightenment. One only has to listen to the stones, feel their vibration, receive their messages to know the secrets. The lessons of greed, dominance, disrespect, and discord also vibrate in the stones of Earth.

Louise has lived much of her current lifetime, within reach of the Appalachian Mountains, which are among the oldest mountains on the planet and predate formation of the North American continent. Pieces of quartz visible to visitors there remind us of the healing stones of Atlantis. From these old mountains, she recalls her experiences of Lemuria and Atlantis.

✳

I see glittery white sandy beaches edging the island of Lemuria, which is isolated from other landmasses by a large expanse of water now known as the Pacific Ocean. The surrounding sea waters lap gently to shore. This peaceful place on the relatively empty planet is the chosen place for my visit. A heavenly place is Lemuria. My materialization occurs at a shiny, metallic receiving portal. I, along with other beings, grace the beaches, floating, swirling, and dancing—images of softness like the clouds moving across the sky from which we came. Our appearance is reminiscent of the Seven Sisters of the Pleiades. The island emanates serenity. The land is lush and Eden-like, the water clear and warm, the air pure.

Our purpose on Lemuria is to set up an energy grid that will radiate the purest and most sacred energy on the planet. This energy field is being set for permanent availability to future Earth civilizations—to have available in the Earth plane the high vibration of purity and clarity.

Before materializing here, I clearly remember standing in front of the highest power and offering to bring a rod of light to the grid. My arm rose without hesitation to be chosen for this work. I love to do good things and I was moved naturally and spontaneously to be a part of this. Spirit says that the grid will be needed when humans live on the planet. The planet will have things and people on it. Life here will be a great challenge. The difficulty of life here will be healed when one connects with the grid of joy.

"They have to want the joy in their hearts," Spirit explains, "and the energy will find them."

"Some will not want the joy?" I ask.

"That is predicted, Miri," I am told.

The planet is alive. Earth is preparing itself to serve the universe this way. The higher energies agreed that the planet can host beings the way it wants to, but in agreeing to this service, the higher energies insisted that the pure energy be made available. It is like a contract, an agreement between Spirit and Earth.

Different rods in the grid come from different high levels of consciousness. Together, they form a scale of sounds carrying the melody of vibration like notes on the staff of the music of life.

I always enjoy a good project. This one fills me with ecstasy, so much so that I stay when the project is complete to dance in joy on the beach. My nymph-like body, wrapped with a filmy, peach-colored drape, alights on the beach and in the clear, blue ocean water. I volunteered for more than this, actually. I agreed, also, to incarnate throughout time to live in the Light and be an example of innocence for the civilizations that establish societies here. My energy mantra always and forever is to *be kind, be compassionate.*

The experience of being a part of this project—preparing a cushion of peace for the coming civilizations—can only compare to a mother preparing a new bassinet with soft, clean white sheets to enfold gently a newborn baby.

No one has to go to the grid to find the energy, even now. It emanates from there. It helps to keep Earth in balance by helping to balance people on Earth. By will alone, this pure ecstatic energy is available to anyone who opens to the possibility of it and draws it in. Long before manifestations of negativity were a reality on the planet, Spirit had planted this endless fountain of purity, heavenly love, and grace for all!

✱

GEORGE: Have you ever been with someone and felt a chill creeping around you like a cloud suddenly blocking the warmth and light of the Sun?

There are two aspects of humankind and two types of energy that evolved from the wondrous beginnings of civilization at

Lemuria. Positive and negative. Light and dark. Kind and cruel. They occur together everywhere on the planet now. Health and disease. Peace and violence. Joy and anger.

Everyone is innately empowered. How everyone discovers and uses their power is their choice, moment by moment. Even the most steadfast carriers of the Light can turn to insensitive, unloving behavior and worse. How deeply someone embraces the purity energy implanted at Lemuria, determines their behavioral choices. When knowledge and avarice and power become primary characteristics stronger than purity, then it is possible to recreate the experience of Atlantis.

Atlantis, the brother civilization of Lemuria, was destroyed by cruelty and greed. Inhabited by highly intelligent beings, Atlantis grew from a pristine island into a futuristic hierarchy of modern buildings, among them temples for healing. This civilization succeeded in harnessing the power of creation and controlling it. Some of the people and places and practices were sacred and pure. Much good came from this. Others took the information further and became heartless and ruthless in their experimentation, causing many innocent people to suffer.

People used stones in highly developed ways for the good of the people: for gentle healing, balancing emotions, increasing energy, increasing conditions for natural fertilization and childbirth, and for other healthful needs.

Stones were also misused in energy experiments to the extent that Earth responded with its own destructive force, putting an end to the entire civilization and reclaiming the land mass for purification.

✳

I see a land where civilization has accomplished greatness, with infrastructure and facilities worthy of an advanced society. All the roadways lead from the shores where the waters lap, up through the enclave of sandstone brick buildings to the pinnacle of facilities at the very top of the mountain island. From a distance, the place has a classical Roman appearance. Close-up, I notice unique engineering.

A tour of the island shows me this. Visiting one temple, I find a multifaceted roof with no visible physical support suspended over a large open area with a 10-ton crystal at the center! The energy received, transmuted, and transmitted by this crystal can be and is used to heal nearly any physical, emotional, or mental imperfection. It connects with the purity grid diametrically opposite on the planet and has an uplifting, elevating effect on those who visit the site. This is heart-based, compassionate healing.

The Keeper of the Crystal is a large, robed woman who carries the responsibility of the healing room squarely on her shoulders as she works with voracious attention to detail. Caring emanates from her every movement.

She does not turn to look at me when she speaks. She is disappointed and angry that I did not follow her advice. When I complain that I am frightened and upset with the new medical procedure I endured, the Keeper merely says, "I warned you what would happen. I told you it would be bad." *What happened to me?* I wonder. *What had I experienced?*

GEORGE: In reply, we encourage her to stick with the memory and look deeper.

I see my family has a quality of contentedness about them. They are in the spice business. Parents, aunts, uncles, and cousins are all involved in gathering plants and preparing spices for sale. The Keeper of the Crystal shops for herbs at the family store. As time passes, I leave the family business and open my own to sell healing herbs and medicinals. The front of my building is a shop, the rear is a laboratory where I experiment with plant life. Inside the shop I see a variety of bottles of prepared medicines for sale.

I appear to be smiling, cheerful, loving, and upbeat with light sandy hair. There is no husband, but there is a young, blond son, maybe six or seven years old. We live together above the shop. There is peacefulness about us.

The sight of my son makes me jump back to the situation that is so difficult to see. My pregnancy is not going as smoothly as I would like. I am not responding to my herbal treatments. I have grown impatient and anxious over the situation. My friend, the Keeper, warns me emphatically not to follow through on my idea to go to the doctors for the modern treatment. They practice mind-over-matter pain management.

I had agreed to have a child seeded in me. My friend, the Keeper, warned me against this. She said the experimenters were evil. That I will suffer and so will the child. My impatience with life, curiosity, and empty arms won out. I did it. I trusted them to be pure of heart.

Now I am able to see the evil lurking behind their faces. I made a mistake and dread floods through my veins.

(My stomach lurches with this recall, my solar plexus shuts down, and I want to flee from this memory. My body knows it is not a good memory.)

It is time for delivery. I walk through a lab to a room with an operating table that resembles a comfortable dentist chair. I lie down and am covered with a white cloth. The head doctor is a short woman; her assistant is a tall man. They approach from behind me. They are icy cold—almost inhuman. She is very serious and determined as she gives her orders. She speaks and he jumps.

I panic. I am in restraints and cannot fight back. Nothing is okay. Everything is wrong. They are using their will. My baby is taken from the belly. I cannot feel any pain, but I sob with fear for what they will do to my baby boy. They immediately take him to another room where they poke him with needles in the heels. He screams in unbearable pain. They are unhappy with his feet and perform surgery without anesthesia.

I continue to hear his horrific wails of pain. The anger of my heartbreak rages. They have no feelings, so they will never understand the pain. *Will my son ever be able to enjoy walking on this Earth,* I wonder.

The Keeper was not unsympathetic, but there was nothing she could do. She had to live with it, too. She reasoned that some people make good medicine and some people make bad medicine.

(Unable to stay with the level of torture wrought on the people, my recall skips forward to the end of that life. Repulsed by the insensitivity of medical and scientific practices, I am barely able to face the consequence that arose.)

My son and I walk on the familiar, local stone street toward our home. This ordinary moment turns tragic. There is rumbling from the ground beneath our feet. The ground shakes and rumbles again. The peace that did exist is broken. The calm of our life turns to trauma. Smoke begins to fill the air from the mountain top behind us. Forces deep within the Earth are pushing up their destruction. Panic fills the streets. People flee, scream, and cry. We cover our faces against the toxic air. My son and I speed up our pace, racing to the shop. We are ahead of the lava flow, but the gases suffuse my senses and time stands still.

My son makes it upstairs ahead of me. I see his feet climbing. He pauses, bends, and turns back to look at me, seeking refuge. It is my last moment. My last memory. His fearful face seeking escape and expecting me to protect him. I have already succumbed to the poisoned air, and lifted from my body, when the scorching lava swallows the limp corpse before eating the stairs and incinerating all evidence of our lives.

With a sudden, fierce explosion of unanticipated magnitude, the top of the island mountain shoots off high into the sky and drops in pieces, spraying the landscape with hot dirt and rocks. The air is dark, littered with fiery rocks, and dense with toxic odors. The rolling liquid surges forth—thick, scorching, and torrid—destroying lives, buildings, infrastructure, animals, plants, and any sign of the life we knew. The sun is obliterated. The land is in darkness, except for fire. The volcano sets off other explosions, fires, and forces. The ground that had always been firm beneath our feet, sought its violent revenge. There is nothing and no one left. This is the cleansing that was feared possible—the end of a civilization.

Suffering is over for now. The pure of heart will set-up another classroom, so the human race can try again to abandon cruelty and maintain balance on the planet.

✳

Just as the insects buzzed earlier in Africa: when Earth gets too out of balance, it destroys and recreates itself of its own material, of its own power, of its own will, in its own nature. *It is not an impossibility.* It will happen again.

My visit to that lifetime ends. I force an exhale and sob tears of sadness and loss and for mistakes made. This memory is a huge burden to bear. The pain suffered by just one newborn innocent and the destruction of *all everyone* finds familiar are unthinkable. There is no one to turn to for help, there is no rescue. There is *no one* at all left on Earth.

The Healing

How do I erase the memory? How do I forgive myself the mistake? How do I erase the experience from my child's memory?

Still Waters stands in front of me now with her hands seemingly as large and white as wings outstretched to me. She says, *Now that you have had this experience, you don't need to experience it again. You are protected and need not fear being led to pain. It is a walk of joy from here on out. Trust us.*

Trust them. Still, my blood boils up and reacts when I visit a doctor in this lifetime. Now I know the source of this reaction. My blood pressure embodies volcano energy, requiring further healing.

I have friends in this lifetime that share this experience. They were part of the advanced medical practices. Their karma from Atlantis is healing and I love them dearly. They stand clearly in the Light now and are precious beings. They were my doctors, and the love between us now wins over anger and grief of that long ago time. The love flows between us.

The experiences of Atlantis can obliterate the joyous experience of Lemuria. To recall the grid of joy and my lack of hesitation in volunteering for a role in living a kind life to help humanity re-centers me in my personal truth. This fitting role calms and focuses me.

My Guides encourage me to spend time alone on the Appalachian Trail. They want me to understand the valuable and powerful, yet safe, help of stones in healing—similar to herbal remedies.

On an early April afternoon I hike a stretch of the Trail in Maryland and quickly discover that spring has arrived in the insect kingdom as the gnats and flies swarm me relentlessly. Up on the ridge, the oak, hickory, and chestnut trees and mountain laurel are still in wintertime, showing little sign of the new life of spring. Butterflies flit up and down the trail and zigzag off into the woods. As I hike alone, the silence is stimulating to my wondering mind. I eventually rest on a large, flat-topped rock where I can see the westward vista and listen to my Guides:

"Mountains watch over life on the planet. Their stones record history. Knowing the stories of your history, you can release the energy of your memories and heal. The stones help you heal.

Let the stones do the healing, even though your own being is crystalline. Use the stones to absorb negative energy that is sent your way or that you absorb. Be like the mountain. Oversee your life, your healing. Be still, calm, solid, and ever so slowly evolving across lifetimes. This is the pace of Earth. Surrender to the stones and stand back, out of the way.

Have patience with yourself and others in healing imbalance and sickness. Allow natural ways to do their job. Observe life like a mountain looking over its valleys.

When your consciousness shifts to be part of the mountain, the gnats that irritate you on the path will disappear. When you realize you are part of everything, nothing can bother you. Be of Earth and for Earth. As you heal, Earth Mother heals also.

Where do you go when you find Oneness, you ask? Achieving Oneness is coming Home."

I did come Home that day. I became the mountain.

My first encounter with healing/helping stones had followed shortly after my first psychic reading with Sara. A specialist in stones gave a presentation locally and I received an invitation. I had no knowledge or understanding of the subject matter, but I was compelled to attend out of open curiosity.

The formal presentation part of the program was a blur—I heard the words that were spoken, but had no way of grounding or organizing the information in my mind. Intellectually, I was lost, but another part of me was hungry and rapt.

Following the presentation, participants formed a circle around a table that was draped and set with a variety of stones that ran the gamut of colors, textures, and sizes. We slowly rotated in the circle around the table with instructions to connect with one stone. *How am I supposed to do that?* I wondered. *I should have paid more attention during the lecture.*

Not since I first met my husband, Jim, and the room shook, have I experienced such a strong vibration of being chosen. A four-to-five-inch-long hunk of yellow crystalline citrine fairly leapt off the table to me! There was no pretending about the connection that zinged me in that instant so clearly that the woman behind me in the circle tapped me on the shoulder and said, "Wow! That stone really wants you!" *Egad! This is awkward! My new friend is a stone.*

The citrine is quite hefty and remains with me today, years later. I like having her around for the strength she emanates—she is *my rock.* The stone's high-pitched, yet firm voice speaks to me:

"Yes, I am for your will—fortitude. Let me help you strengthen your resolve. There is nothing that you cannot do. Will your life into being. Make it yours, all yours. Release your uniqueness for the world to see. Do not muddle and suppress yourself any more. There is nothing to fear. Adopt this new attitude of freedom. Firm up your soft underbelly that has stored your hesitation and fear. Toughen up. Be strong. Be sure of yourself. Step up and be seen and heard. Give free reign to your creativity. Beneath your feet is courage. Within you is a heart of crystal. Above you is Divine love. Fear not."

"Yes, ma'am," I respond. "I will attempt to do that!" Such words of encouragement one rarely hears!

When I first visited the Grand Canyon with Jim and Matt, temperatures were cold; snow mixed with rain; the trail was slippery underfoot; and dramatic views of canyon walls and endless space could be quickly spied between low, blowing clouds. Much of the canyon's splendor remained hidden. It was a short visit—a brief introduction—awesome and teasing. Millions of years of Earth's history recorded in the strata of the Canyon walls, thanks to the artistic, eroding forces of the Colorado River.

I returned to this magnificent place in summer with Sandy and hiked alone under the wide blue sky and the hot sun. Stepping slowly on the Bright Angel Trail, I savored each moment. Numerous other hikers moved along at an athletic clip and some passed me again on their return trip to the top while I was still descending near the rim of the great abyss.

While many seemed to be conquering the canyon, I was open to connecting with it. The strata of rock are a study in time. Resting against the canyon wall below the rim, I had a meditative moment with another's voice. It was my brother, who was on the other side, and he was delighted for my accomplishment of making it to this grand place. He had not visited here while he was alive, and he rejoiced in being here with me at this time. "Isn't this amazing?" I exclaimed to him. "It sure is, Weezer," he replied, calling me by my childhood nickname. And I knew instinctively, he was traveling with me and we would be together again in travels across the web of time.

The canyon rumbled and shook me. A vibration ran up through my legs. No one else seemed to feel it. Three rocks broke loose nearby. They dropped by my feet. The dusty sandstone chunks fit into my pockets. The canyon spoke! I felt it! I was enthralled by this communion with Earth—or was it my brother teasing me, like old times?

Later, I meditated with each of the stones. The Spirit of one of them is Destiny-Time and spoke this message to me:

"I broke off the Canyon wall for you. I want to be with you for all time. You understand the past, present, and future of living," (My head itched and legs chilled. Then chills ran all over my body.) Destiny-Time continued, "I will accompany you to your destiny. I will keep you on track and protect you."

Destiny-Time is one among many stones in my collection now.

Rediscovery of the voice of Spirit in stones and the joy of healing with stones are liberating gifts that had been lost to me in the agony of Atlantis—wisdom petrified and sunken beyond reach. Resurrecting the power of stones and reconnecting to the grid of joy awakens the music of the soul, taking me Home to my core essence and purpose. The vibration of joy resonates in an uninterrupted rhythm, working to dislodge all pain and suffering of living and dying over the ages. Joy dances in the body, bubbling and frolicking in its natural celebratory dance.

Yes, there is a lot to learn—stones, plants, and animals are here to help and heal us! They teach wisdom that unlocks doors to enlightenment. The future lies within me and within these connections. Fear not, look inside, and there it will be!

George's Interlude

Dear Reader, let me share an allegorical story with you regarding the hard work required to reach a goal:

The path of gray gravel stones was rough and uneven underfoot. It was difficult for the woman to maintain balance while negotiating this trail. Gray dust kicked up and drifted down to thinly coat her shoes. She had walked quite a ways on this path. Suddenly, she stopped, noticing ahead of her a large, gray boulder blocking her way. A light and gentle arm wrapped around her shoulders, encouraging her to continue moving forward to the rock. She glimpsed that it was the friendly figure's other hand that had just placed the boulder on her path! His touch on her shoulder was loving, and the boulder was placed with the same compassionate touch. This she did not like. *What kind of trick is this*, she wondered. Love should not bring challenges, she thought. *Love should be only easy. But this was apparently not the case!* She had to let go of the anger that rose in her.

The figure spoke, "You are not to fly over it this time. You are to move through it."

"Why," she asked, "would I put myself through the ordeal of trying to go through this thing when it's easier to go over it?" There was no response. She was left to make her own choices. This woman did not like failing, yet she was just not courageous enough to accomplish this.

She touched the rock and felt its solidity. She entered the rock and felt its oppressiveness. She climbed on top of it and saw on the other side that the gravel path became a rich and green grassy meadow dotted with a multitude of colorful flowers.

I must do this, she told herself. *I must do this, this time.* The days and months passed as she nearly succeeded at her challenge. Every time she entered the stone, she could not breathe and could not stay long enough to break through to the other side.

Much time passed. No matter how many diversions she had found over the years, the stone would not disappear. She accepted that this stone was the center of her existence, because it was.

The figure that had left her with the stone returned. He said, "You must learn to focus. Use all your will power, all your physical strength, and your mental determination to focus on going through the stone." She was relieved to hear some advice, but this was not the advice she wanted to hear—it just took too much effort. It required her to be strong where she was weak.

What he's saying, she thought, *is I really have to get it together. My will, will replace self-doubt and fear. Strength will overcome my weaknesses, of which there are a few. Determination will be the glue that holds together my scattered, nervous nature.*

It took much more practice. She really did not like to focus on what she preferred to ignore, but slowly she began to surrender rather than resist. This is the hard work of reaching through fears and apprehensions necessary to heal.

She entered the stone and moved with commitment and determination into the very center of the stone. There she lingered, looked around, and let herself experience the painful emptiness of this dead place. The nothingness felt sickening, repulsive, nauseating. *This is the seed of disease*, she realized.

She kept breathing and forced herself to keep going. She did not turn back. As she moved on, it did not get worse as she had feared. It did not get worse! It was just more of the same dead space. *I have seen the worst! There is nothing worse!* With this revelation, she sensed she was almost through and burst out the other side.

She stepped forth into the light and stood with her feet upon the soft, green earth for which she had yearned. Joyous elements of the air surrounded her in celebration—butterflies, dragonflies, birds. She was free. She danced among the flowers in the bright light of day. Looking back she noticed the boulder had broken and fallen into sections that lay awkward and askew, rocking on rounded curves or sitting on flat edges. She chuckled at them and continued on her way, moving from one pretty flower to the next.

Along her new path of freedom she meets many wonderful people and is very grateful to have learned her lesson. The people she meets share their love with her; and because she freed her heart of oppression, she discovered the love that lives within her and is able to share it with others. Welcome Home!

ॐ

PART III
ARRIVING HOME

14

Gifts from the Light

My HERB AND MEDITATION GARDEN, my refuge, is in the full sun of the day. I sit among the plants, absorbing the sun, too. The treasured lavender (*Lavendula angustifolia*) and delicate meadow rue (*Thalictrum spp*) are separated by a path of stepping-stones that is lined with thyme (*Thymus serpyllum*). Red bee balm (*Monarda didyma*), columbine (*Aquilegia caerulea*), and black-eyed Susans (*Rudbeckia divergens*) are in full bloom with a scattering of happy, white Queen Anne's lace (*Daucus carota*) that has invaded the borders. They are one of my favorites and remind me of my childhood, picking wildflowers from the fields near my house. They seem comically miniature now after confronting the tall cow parsnip (*Heracleum lanatum*) in Black Rain's meadow!

Mint (*Mentha arvensis*) and wild strawberries (*Frageria vesca*) proliferate, because there is no stopping their invasive natures. In the pond, fast-growing lotus buds (*Mrs. Perry Slocum Nelumbo*) emerge from the water. They will grow taller and fuller; open for a showy, awesome display; and then be done for the season—all within several days.

In some cultures, the lotus is a symbol of enlightenment. For me, its roots in the muddy bottom of the pond represent the muck and mire of life on Earth. Its home, a pond, represents the emotional waters requiring work, will, and determination to tame in healing. The glorious opening to full bloom high in the air under the midsummer sun is synonymous with the fruition of reaching for higher understanding to full freedom.

Glancing around, I see the sweet honeysuckle (*Diervilla lonicera*), common dandelions (*Taraxacum officinale*), and oily poison ivy (*Toxicodendron radicans*) that seemingly thrive wherever I live.

The Latin genus and species of these plants is scientific knowledge gleaned from field guides and field studies with local naturalists that balance and ground my spiritual connection to Nature. The names of plant families, identification of habitats, and uses for plants demonstrate some of the ways humanity has worked to understand nature around us.

A simple, unmarked golden butterfly—that could be a Cloudless Sulphur (*Phoebis sennae*)—drifts down to me and lands trustingly on my right arm. Wondering how long he will stay, I sit perfectly still. He strokes me gently with his left antenna, rests, and flies off. My thoughts take wing with the trusting butterfly, a symbol of transformation. *Even the most ferocious of wildlife are concerned with their safety, and so am I. So, my question to you, Spirit, is what is my protection?*

My mind drifts off. I travel out of my body and become like a wispy cloud—white, soft, weightless, and free. Rising over the Earth I find Christ, Buddha, and the other Ascended Masters. Even though they each have separate names, religions, pathways, and groups here on Earth, I notice their energies are similar. They appear to be together where their pathways merge into a ring of Light.

I look down at Earth from this higher perspective. Increasing gradations of darkness appear the closer to Earth I look—denser and denser layers of pollution—from the encircling ring of purity high above down through rings of grayness. On Earth occurs the darkest ring of all—a place of heavy energy and emotions. I compare this to the purity of the Light.

I realize we have many paths to choose to reach the summit—this ring of Light. My journey leads to you. Some trails are long and gentle; others steep and short; and many trails intersect, offering us choices of which path to take. Lingering, I retrieve this message from the beings of the Light:

"Are you seeking answers to questions regarding purpose, place, and time? Regarding what is possible and the *whys, what ifs,* and *how coulds* pertaining to the world around you? We suggest you focus on the question of *who.* Seek answers to questions regarding who you are. When you do experience who you are, you automatically know the important ingredients for creating a full, good life. *Shift your focus from studying the creation of the world to the life you are creating!*

Find the doorway to enlightenment within your being and unlock it. You will find *us* there and more. Wisdom is the key that unlocks the door from the physical world to spiritual realms.

There are many ways to reach enlightenment, which is the honorable goal of your striving. Allow yourself to experience the magnificence of the Universe and the Universal aspect of your being. You have permission to do this, the power to do this, and need only the will to do this—it is up to you. We see the unenlightened as:

Seeds struggling to bud,
Birds with broken wings,

Vessels kept empty,
Songs left unsung,

The beauty of the Universe
Denied the light of day.

Closed minds, closed hearts,
Lost along the way.

Think of what you are creating in your life, rather than what you do for a living. What is building as a result of your actions? The answer to that question is where you are headed. When you think of your actions as part of creating life, they take on new purpose and meaning.

Remember you only have to uncover the secrets of your past experiences to understand your present situation. The answers lie within you, and await your discovery and outward expression.

Bud to bloom,
Wing in flight,
Man enlightened.
Open mind, open heart,
Flowing on Earth,
Like water
Connecting all.

Seek your personal power for yourself. Seek not to have power over others. Allow yourself to flow across this lifetime and over all times. Accept all the good that surrounds you and let it flow out to others. We are thrilled to see you seeking and searching. We are jubilant to see you reaching within and beyond your usual ways. The journey is the thrill!"

I descend back through these levels to my body in the garden. It is a startlingly tight fit! I have expanded! The body takes away the freedom of my Spirit. I am uncomfortable, heavier, and restricted. The farthest outside edges of my aura press out against the Earthly darkness. I am a glowing light in the darkness. My glow, my good energy, is strong enough to withstand the darkness around me and it lights up my space!

You do not need to contain your spirit energy within the tight fitting body, Spirit explains. *You can release it like breath through the body.*

Oh, good! When I physically exhale, this brings relief similar to peeling off a pair of control-top pantyhose on a 100-degree day. I breathe through my body, rather than within it.

Black Rain appears in front of me and shows me within his hands a large flat piece of clear and white crystal resembling a sheet of ice from the surface of a stream, etched with frost and crystalline patterns. As he places the crystalline plate into the head of my energy body, my left hand chills. "This gift," he says, "symbolizes the crystalline nature of your being."

Still Waters appears and hands me a gift of bright yellow hair with two long braids. "This is the essence of your golden and abundant beauty," she says. The nature of one's hair, some say, is the measure of one's spiritual strength. My belief in myself surges with satisfaction— the struggle is over. *I made it!*

George appears and places a small bird on my shoulder, symbolizing the new peace and winged freedom of my spirit. "It is you who set yourself free," he says, "It is you who earned this. The world is waiting. They will hear you this time. Your words will be heard and you will be at peace. At the passing of this lifetime in about 20 years after your major accomplishments, you will look back at a job well done, a life lived well."

I breathe heavily with the joy, excitement, and satisfaction from the spiritual connections and understanding indicated by these very great gifts from my devoted Spirit Guides. Their support and devotion awe me. I am smiling, smiling, smiling.

An image of a hand reaches out and turns on the faucet of a pipeline. The flow of power begins in my lower body and chills rise up through my spine. My energy is awakened and vibrates up through me.

Will these gifts heal my fear of dying at the whim of a fickle crowd? Somehow, will the crowd be pleased now?

I ask, again, for a symbol of protection to quell the fear in me once and for all. Something I can trust and rely on, for now my fear has grown into fear of fear, also. As the earlier vision of my Spirit glowing reappears, I take several new, deep breaths, unlike any breaths I have taken before. I inhale pure white light through the top of my head and bring it all the way into my physical body. This breath is full. This is the breath of life force. *Your protection,* a voice answers my questions, *is your Light, your wholeness. Breathe it in.*

Still Waters has another gift for me, a colorful sash. Ceremoniously, she drapes it over my outstretched hands and tells me it is the sash of the Rainbow Woman, a sacred sash with all the colors of the rainbow that represent wholeness and unity. "Wear it proudly, my child," she says and fades away. The meditation ends.

I am giddy with childlike happiness. Excitement dances through me. I have my answers to healing and protection. I am at One with the Universe in my plant and rock garden, Earth, no longer defined by the fear and limitations of past existences. When all is said and done, all there is, is One.

15

Live Consciously

THERE ARE MANY WAYS TO die, many ways to live. To live consciously, consider these exercises:

1. Think positively—what you believe about yourself is your best protection.

2. Never say "hate" and know that what you put out to the world is what returns to you.

3. Seek the invisible aspect of life, for therein lies the secrets and magic of living and dying.

4. Spend time in nature and surround yourself with life force.

5. Dare to analyze your life strategy and identify which lessons you are mastering in this lifetime (anger, hatred, jealousy, fear, evil, poverty, handicap, etc.). Work to accomplish the lessons.

6. In your new life strategy, set others free. Do not think that if they are working on a lesson different from yours (for instance, you are wealthy and someone else is in poverty), that they are less worthy. Honor each being for their role in the world and the role they play in your life. Each person of

poverty has the opportunity to learn self-worth, which in turn provides the opportunity for others to learn value. Earth is a school; life is the lesson.

7. Pray big. Make the leap to praying for all humans, the planet, the waterways, and peace. Pray especially for the water and use it to spread sentiments of love and gratitude across the planet.

George's Final Interlude
A Meditation on Life

Reader, feel yourself in a ray of the Sun with the solar warmth penetrating your body. Observe yourself as a speck of Light on the face of Earth that floats among other planets, space, stars, vast dark areas, and wrinkles in space and time unknown to you. From this higher perspective, see yourself as part of the bigger landscape that houses, nurtures, and supports you.

There is a bigger picture of life than what you have been taught. Parts of Earth have been populated many times during the eons. The human race today is nearing the platforms of achievement reached many times in the past by previous civilizations. Do you remember? Have you been there? When a civilization experiences all that it can within the boundaries and limitations of its host planet, the civilization vanishes. This has been true many times on Earth. When the momentum of the advancement of civilization reaches the edge, civilization follows. Where does it go? Into another dimension.

The consciousness of the civilization is what lives on, moving from manifestation to manifestation, refinement to refinement, providing a balance to populations in different places on this planet, on other planets, and anywhere.

Understand that part of you lives in your physical Earth body and other aspects of you (your consciousness) live in other places at the same time. You are connected to the Sun, the stars, the Moon, planets beyond, and dimensions that exist contiguously with you today. Many people are aware of the physical body, the energy body, and the emotional/etheric body around them. Now imagine that there are additional aspects of you located beyond the visible physical dimension.

Discovering the full, true identity of your being is the undercurrent of living. What is your history on Earth? When have you lived? Where have you lived? What did you learn from these experiences? What excess emotion do you hold onto from these experiences?

Are you using your talents and abilities? Do you know what your talents and abilities are, and have you looked for new ones lately? Are you willing to expand the definition of yourself continuously? What are you becoming—taking shape like gelatin becoming set in the form of a mold, or taking shape as in growing wings?

Shed the cloak of modern life, reconnect with the Earth, discover your personal creativity within, and from this center create your life anew moment by moment.

Clean out the negative memories. They are negatively charged and attract only negative experiences. The past is past, so complete it. Shift the content of what you carry around. You have the power to create and recreate your life continuously and create a higher consciousness for your future. This is important.

Your success in resolving the past relates to your ability to accomplish your life's purpose. It is necessary to pass through the veil of illusions and limitations. Allow all your talents and abilities to come forth—all your creativity and magnetism.

There are other choices for everything. Some are liberating, expressive, perpetual, and endowing. Try making love differently, eating differently, exercising differently, meditating differently. Choose a way that you think might be better for you—ones that would be more rewarding and bring more energy to you.

What if you admitted you don't know it all and gave up your know-it-all attitude? Feel how much energy it takes to hold that attitude in place. No one knows it all. Do not waste your energy thinking you have to. If you are living a life of expanding awareness, you will find that times of great personal achievement are followed by humble times of being a novice.

When your attitude toward yourself is open, courageous, and

compassionate, the joy of wholeness and Oneness can flow into you. Open to all of yourself and embrace it. Be it. Live it. Reach beyond your old self-definitions and self-limitations to greater fulfillment.

The common thread of all our lives is Earth. She is everywhere beneath our feet—in dust and desert, in jungle and forest, on open plains, in deep caves, and on island land masses. Reconnect with Earth and accomplish your life's purpose.

Open your eyes, be aware, awaken.

ℬℛ

_____

The End

LOUISE MITCHELL CONTINUES HER JOURNEY, exploring the sacred quality of life and finding the source of joy all around her in nature. Living in the foothills of the Colorado Rocky Mountains with her family, she is a spiritual mentor and conducts meditation workshops where participants translate meditations into shield art imbued with energy for their personal growth.

Louise has a degree in art history and studied natural history, environmental issues, and Native culture.

She is President of Evergreen Mountain Writers. Her background includes non-fiction writing and editing of newspaper columns, newsletters, a magazine, and marketing publications.

To learn more about her programs, to purchase a workbook for self-study of *Feet Upon the Earth*, or to visit with the author, go to: www.LaughingWatersWay.com.